100
GREAT CITIES
OF WORLD HISTORY

Chrisanne Beckner

A Bluewood Book

Published in 1995 by
Bluewood Books
A Division of The Siyeh Group, Inc.,
P.O. Box 460313
San Francisco, CA 94146

ISBN 0-912517-14-X

Printed in the USA

Edited by Bill Yenne
and Sarah Krall

Designed and captioned by
Ruth DeJauregui

Cover illustration by
Vadim Vahrameev

About the author:
   Chrisanne Beckner is a writer living in San Francisco, California. *100 Great Cities of World History* is her first book.

TABLE OF CONTENTS

10.
26.

9.
54. **50.**   **4.**

3,000 BC   **1800 BC**

44.

7.
93. 75. 72.

42.
65.

1800 BC

600 BC

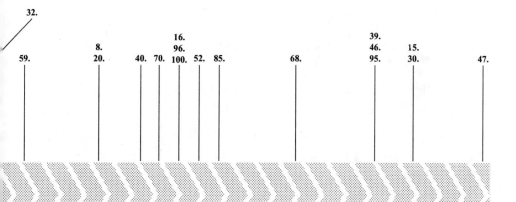

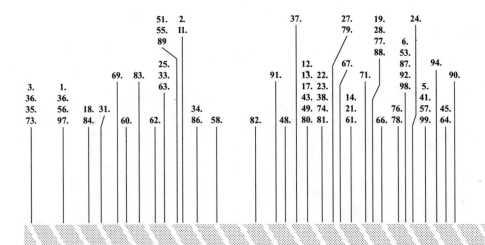

800 AD

2000 AD

INTRODUCTION

The cities of the world are central points in the story of human history. The heads of government have plotted wars from within their ancient walls. Their museums have collected the finest evidence of human creativity. Their institutions chronicle the values of civilizations throughout time. From Vatican City within Rome to the once abandoned ruins of Machu Picchu, it is the world's great cities that preserve the history of human evolution. This book explores the riches of 100 of these cities.

Chosen for the almost undefinable quality of greatness, these cities together act as a sort of chronological, geographical map through the world's most admired civilizations. From Damascus, Syria, thought to be the oldest city still inhabited, to American, Canadian and African cities almost as young as Tel Aviv, Israel (1909), these 100 cities have seen the people and events that define history.

Athens, Greece saw the birth of the Western World, was home to Socrates, Plato, and Homer, and maintains the relics that defined art and architecture for the West. Rome's empire rose and fell on the current site where the original roads still function. Relics of the Roman forum still stand. On the banks of the Nile River, ancient Cairo has continued to flourish next to the temples of pharaohs and the ancient "City of the Dead." In America, Washington, DC maintains the Smithsonian Museums, the world's largest museum complex.

Though each city has a unique history, a style as distinct as a fingerprint, these chosen 100 share some of the same attributes. Almost all have been centers for either commercial, political or cultural power. They've existed as magnets for great people, great heroism, and great ingenuity. Many of them rose to power after the Industrial Revolution. Others have long histories of empirical power, and empirical personalities. Each of them has developed an architectural style that aesthetically defines the values of a culture. Each also has a chronological lifetime including a series of events that can be viewed as a distinct history, as well as a piece of a world history puzzle.

Together, these places create a picture of human civilizations. Their evolution can be compared, contrasted and explored. One can note that Napoleon crowned himself Emperor of France from Paris's Notre Dame (1804) at the same time that South America was pulling away from Spanish rule. One can plot wars, empires and religious trends. Above all, one can celebrate the enormity of human experience and human endeavor.

Panorama of the Forum, the heart of Rome. Known as the "Eternal City," Rome is civilization's archetypical metropolis.

ALGIERS, ALGERIA
Founded in the tenth century

Algiers, **Algeria's** capital, chief seaport, political center and cultural base, was also the home of the infamous **Barbary pirates** of the sixteenth through the nineteenth centuries. **Barbarossa**, a Turkish corsair who seized Algiers for the **Ottoman Empire** in 1529, freed the island of **Penon** from the Spaniards, as the Emir of Algiers had requested. He then gathered the Moors, who had been expelled from Spain, into a pirate force that ruled the seas and struck fear into the hearts of all European traders on the Mediterranean. In 1830, the French finally captured Algiers and crippled the pirate forces, turning the Turkish city into a military base for their growing control over North and West Africa. But for the 300 years prior, the city of Algiers had flourished under Barbarossa's governance.

Although Barbarossa's legendary ruthlessness was rumored all over Europe, he was an excellent leader. His prisoners were allowed relative freedom within the city, where they were treated much like Algerian citizens. Prisoners were the main commodity of the Turkish pirates, as their labor built the dazzling white buildings facing the Mediterranean Sea. The city rose from its obscure origins as a Phoenician North African colony and spread out over the slopes of the Sahel Hills and the islands off the coast (all but one of which have been attached to the mainland by reclamation.) Many vain attempts were made to destruct the piracy, including naval expeditions by the Holy Roman Emperor **Charles**

V in 1541 and by the British, Dutch and Americans in the early 1800s. These attacks weakened Algiers' dominance, but did not destroy it until France's final attack in 1830, which ended the powerful, almost mythological, force of the pirate age.

Algeria rose up against French rule in the 1950s and gained independence in 1962. Many Europeans fled in the following decades, leaving the city to the Islamic population. Today Algiers is still growing, its population having reached 1.7 million in 1990.

The old section of the city, built on the upper slopes of the hills, still retains its early character, identified by high, blank-walled houses and narrow, winding streets. The famous **Kasbah** still dominates the Muslim section of town and was the residence of the last two **Turkish deys** in Algiers. The **Ketchaoua Mosque**, which was the **Cathedral of St. Philip** from 1845 to 1962, is still a prominent landmark, and the **Museum of Popular Arts and Traditions** is housed in one of the finest Turkish palaces ever built.

A panoramic view of Algiers, circa 1940.

Amsterdam, with its distinctive red brick residences and elaborate network of canals, is the nominal capital of **The Netherlands**, although it yields the government seat to **The Hague**. The **Royal Palace** is rarely inhabited by the Royal Family, and the city lacks the noble architectural wonders and grand squares that Europe's great capitals feature. What the city does have is a rich heritage as one of the world's major ports and commercial centers since the sixteenth century. It has an international reputation for tolerance and wildly progressive ideas as well as a creative, cosmopolitan collection of young citizens.

The city sits at the mouth of the **Ij**, an inland arm of the former **Zuiderzee**, and is divided by the canalized **Amstel River**. The old medieval city covers both banks of the Amstel in the city's center and is surrounded by the **Singel** (canal). Here, much remains the same. The narrow streets are still lined by gabled houses and brick facades, twenty percent of the 713,000 residents still use bicycles for transportation, and the canals which run between seventeenth and eighteenth century patrician houses are still lined with houseboats.

The city still has an old Jewish quarter, where the Portuguese Synagogue was built in 1670. Amsterdam's worst loss in **World War II** was the 70,000 Jewish residents who were deported to concentration camps. Among them was **Anne Frank**, whose diary remains a testament to the spirit of the many Jewish people who were forced into hiding.

Amsterdam is world renowned for its booming **diamond industry**, and it is one of Europe's most powerful financial and commercial centers. Amsterdam has prospered as such since the seventeenth century, when the **Amsterdam Exchange Bank** (1609) became the largest clearinghouse in Europe.

Amsterdam was the site of the **1928 Olympic Games** and was known then for the color of its working class suburbs, where flowers could be seen in every window. The city is blessed with excellent museums, including the **Rijksmuseum**, famous for its collection of the seventeenth century Dutch masters, and the **Stedelijk Museum**, featuring modern artists like **Picasso** and **Chagall**, **Matisse** and **Rauschenberg**. Indeed, the greatest Dutch painter of all, **Rembrandt van Rijn**, lived here in the mid-seventeenth century and his home is itself preserved as a museum. The **Van Gogh Museum** opened in 1972, and the city is full of currently producing artists, musicians, authors and actors.

A copper weathervane overlooks Amsterdam's skyline. This swan stands on the dome of the Renaissance Hotel.

Capital of the **Khmer (Cambodian) Empire** from the ninth to the fifteenth centuries, the city of **Angkor** was abandoned after Thai armies sacked it in 1431. The city's skeleton remains an excellent site, albeit recently war-damaged, to study the highly sophisticated culture that once lived and worshiped there.

Conceived as a religious center based on Indian principles of cosmology, the city was built around a central monument on the hill **Phnom Bakheng**. The many elegant monuments around it were centers for the worship of both Indian mythological figures and the monarch, who was seen as the embodiment of immortal gods and goddesses. Through the remains of the city's greatest period of construction, which lasted over 300 years, changes in architecture and worship can be traced. While the temples, highly carved and ornamented, were originally tied to the Hindu god **Siva**, they later served the god **Vishnu** and then a **Mahayana Buddhist sect** that worshiped the bodhisattva **Avalokitesvara**.

The most famous of these temples, **Angkor Wat**, where **Suryavarman II** was worshiped and entombed as the god Vishnu, remained fairly complete, even after Thai armies on the empire's western outskirts began spreading into Khmer heartland. The Khmer cults had slowed their building in favor of a more restrained Buddhist lifestyle. The **Theravada Buddhist monks** managed to save Angkor Wat and maintain it after the city's fall, which led to later curiosity about the lost city that seemed to retreat into the **Cambodian** forest.

In 1863, when the French colonial regime took Angkor over, scholarly interest brought a group of French archaeologists here to uncover the city's history and attempt to restore its ancient temples. Along with the monuments, all of which were religious in nature and dedicated to the Khmer kings, many reservoirs, canals and moats were discovered, enhancing the belief that the populace was exceptionally advanced and prosperous.

Contemporary wars have once again endangered the site, as has thievery and long-term neglect, and the jungle threatens to swallow Angkor again.

A detail of the fabulous carvings ornamenting the temple of Angkor Wat.

The undisputed mother of Western culture, ancient **Athens** was an incomparable, irreplaceable apex of thought, creativity and political insight. **Greece's** golden age, from 457 BC to 429 BC, saw the city grow into the world's model for the arts and architecture. During this era, **Ictinus** and **Callicrates** built the **Parthenon** on the **Acropolis**, while **Phidia** completed one of the seven wonders of the ancient world, the **statue of Zeus** at Elis, and **Pericles** strengthened Athens for the **Peloponnesian War** with Sparta. Pericles was the student of the philosopher **Anaxagoras**, the first man to introduce a dualistic explanation of the universe by stating that all objects are composed of small particles, or atoms. At the same time, Athenian doctors were rejecting the idea that disease was unaccountable or a punishment from the gods, thus scientific medicine was born. **Socrates** developed the **Socratic method**, a question and answer method of teaching. His developments inspired students like **Plato**, who wrote *The Republic* and schooled **Aristotle**, who in turn wrote the equally powerful *Politics* and schooled **Alexander the Great**.

Athens' golden age ended in 429 BC with a plague that killed both Pericles and one-third of the city's population. However, the city continued to produce masters of art and science. Here playwrights, like **Aeschylus, Euripides** and **Sophocles**, competed in annual theater competitions held as early as the fifth century BC. Their works survive and continue to influence even the modern film industry. Here the **Olympic Games** began at nearby **Mt. Olympus'** foot in 776 BC. Here the blind poet **Homer** composed the *Iliad* and *Odyssey* in 850 BC. These works encompass so much human heroism in the face of the gods' will that they served as basic educational texts, remaining timeless and inviting even today.

The remaining monuments, which speak of Athenian greatness, are world treasures that were built in an atmosphere of creativity, scientific exploration and intellectual debate. The **Acropolis** houses the Parthenon, which, it has been said, is "as deceptively simple as Socrates' conversation; this columned, oblong temple is the expression — without a trace of strain or conflict — of a human ideal of clarity and unity."

Athens is a city of 748,000 living in 165 square miles (427 square kilometers) on the Kifisos River and the Ilisos rivers. When Greece, absorbed by the Ottoman Empire in the fifteenth century, became a constitutional monarchy in 1833, Athens once again was made the capital of Greece, a role it retained when Greece became a republic after **World War II**.

The ruins of the Acropolis overlook modern Athens.

Atlanta, Georgia's elegant capital and largest city, covering an area of 132 square miles (342 square kilometers), is the Southern center of politics, communications, finance and commerce. Many international industrial giants, like **Coca-Cola**, founded in Atlanta in 1886, have their headquarters here, as do government agencies, like the **Centers for Disease Control** and the **Sixth Federal Reserve District**. The site of the **1996 Olympic Games**, the city is also a major educational center for the southeast. **Atlanta University** was established in 1865, **Clark College**, in 1869, and **Emory University**, in 1836. Georgia Institute of Technology (1888), or **Georgia Tech**, is another of the more than twenty secondary institutions attended by students from Atlanta's population of 394,000.

In 1837, the city's site was chosen as a terminus for a new railroad bound for **Chattanooga, Tennessee**. Named first **"Terminus,"** and later **"Marthasville,"** for the daughter of **Governor Wilson Lumpkin** (1834), it was renamed Atlanta at its incorporation as a city, in honor of the **Western & Atlantic Railroad** (1845).

During the **Civil War**, **General William Tecumseh Sherman** targeted Atlanta because it was a major supplier for the **Confederate** army. After capturing the city in the **Battle of Atlanta** (1864), he used it as a military camp and then departed on November 15 for his famous "march to the sea." The city, left in ashes, was rebuilt and chosen to be a federal political center.

As Atlanta matured into a business center, relations with the North were repaired. Three expositions marked the city's new identity as a leader of **"the New South."** The **International Cotton Exposition** was held in 1881, the **Piedmont Exposition**, in 1887, and the **Cotton States and International Exposition**, in 1895. It was then that **Booker T. Washington** gave his famous and controversial speech for black citizens. He agreed that blacks could be pulled from government and politics as long as educational and technical training were provided to black citizens interested in self-education and personal responsibility.

From this point on, Atlanta was a fiery center for the black civil rights movement. Although Atlanta was the first city to integrate its schools without major disturbances and the first big Southern city to elect a black mayor (1973), it also had riots in 1966 and 1967, when the **Civil Rights Movement** was gaining power and support throughout the nation. **Martin Luther King, Jr.'s Southern Christian Leadership Conference** was headquartered in Atlanta, and his body is buried in the **Ebenezer Baptist Churchyard**.

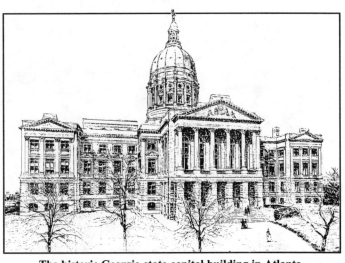

The historic Georgia state capital building in Atlanta.

In the eighth and ninth centuries, **Baghdad** was considered the richest city in the world. Traders from China, India and East Africa crossed paths here, exchanging cultural delicacies and coaxing Baghdad into an intellectual renaissance. Hospitals and an observatory were built; poets and artisans were nurtured; and Greek masterpieces were translated into Arabic.

A Thousand and One Nights, including the famous tales of **Sinbad**, encapsulates the cultural brevity of Baghdad during its reign as the acknowledged leader of the Arab and Muslim worlds.

The medieval city of Baghdad was built by the **Abbasid caliph al-Mansur**, second caliph of the **Abbasid Dynasty**, across both the east and west banks of the **Tigris River**. Encircled with three fortifying walls, the city was divided into four equal quarters, with four main roads leading from the caliph's palace to the grand mosque and out into greater **Iraq**. Covering roughly two miles on the east bank between the gates of **al-Mu'azzam Square** in the north and **ash-Sharqui Square** in the south, ancient Baghdad still can be recognized in the **Abbasid Palace**, from the late twelfth or thirteenth centuries, in the bazaars, full of copper and gold, and in the mosques and public baths, built during the four centuries of **Ottoman** rule (1535 to 1918).

From its zenith under the Abbasid caliphs, the city began to weaken in the tenth century. Spoiled crops and internal strife led to its vulnerability. Sacked by the Mongols, under **Hulagu Khan**, grandson of **Genghis Khan**, in 1258, Baghdad was then taken by the Ottoman Turks, who included Baghdad as part of the empire in 1535.

After the fall of the Ottoman Empire in 1918, European influence changed the face of the city. By 1920, Baghdad, which had grown from its original enclosed center to 254 square miles (657 square kilometers), became the capital of the new state of Iraq. The worldwide need for oil gave Baghdad a new power in the international economy of the 1970s. Under the rule of strongman **Saddam Hussein**, Iraq undertook ill-fated wars against Iran in the 1980s and Kuwait in 1990. The latter resulted in the **Persian Gulf War** of 1991, which led to massive air-raids against Baghdad's transportation and communications infrastructure.

As of 1990, the city of Baghdad had a growing population of 4.6 million, as compared to only 180,000 in 1890.

The Kadhimain Mosque of Baghdad, circa 1930.
This is where the faithful pray according to the tenets of the Koran. Note the classic architecture of the domes and four minarets.

BANGKOK, THAILAND
Founded in 1782

Bangkok, the capital and chief port of **Thailand**, is internationally known for its native serenity and its peoples' deference and politeness. Considered a city made sinful by the overabundance of sensual pleasures, Bangkok has attracted the world's greatest pleasure seekers. Even its name tantalizes the senses; Bangkok means "the village of wild plums."

Located on the delta of the **Chao Phraya River**, about 25 miles north of the Gulf of Thailand, Bangkok is 20 times larger than the next biggest Thai city. Criss-crossed with canals which commonly flood, the city has grown past its original walls to encompass the surrounding area's luscious, agricultural land. The inner city, where the eighteenth century **Grand Palace** once housed government offices, now hosts the city's businesses and over 300 Buddhist temples. Called wats, these structures, which are located throughout Bangkok, feature gold ornamentation, burnished copper domes, glass mosaics and Chinese ceramics. Warehouses have been constructed on both banks of the river, and a floating market functions between them, selling fresh produce and handmade goods.

The city was formerly divided into two municipalities connected by several bridges — **Krung Thep** on the east bank and **Thon Buri** on the west — until 1971, when Bangkok was united into one city-province. The metropolis now has a 604 square mile (1,565 square kilometers) area that was inhabited by 5.9 million people in 1990, as compared to 200,000 in 1890. Bangkok's population is exceptional because two-fifths of the residents are under twenty years old, and one-fifth is under thirty. Restrictive foreign immigration quotas adopted after **World War II** have kept the number of non-Thai residents at under three percent, ensuring Bangkok's distinctive character.

Bangkok became the capital of **Siam** (now Thailand) in 1782, when the ruling **Chakri Dynasty's** founder, who took the name **Rama I**, moved the court from the west to the east bank. **Rama II** (1809-1824) and **Rama III** (1824-1851) built more wats, which, in addition to being religious centers, were used as schools, hospitals and recreation areas. **Rama IV** improved the Grand Palace, built impressive royal homes and laid several new streets, while **Rama V** (1868-1910) developed a public works program, which created an ancillary garden city and many roads and bridges to accommodate cars' increasing popularity. **Rama VI** (1910-1925) established **Chulalongkorn University** (1916) and a system of locks to control waterways throughout the city.

A typical Thai floating market.

Within the autonomous region of **Spain** called **Catalonia**, **Barcelona**, the capital, acts as a living gallery of modernist and **Art Nouveau** architecture and decor. The temples and buildings of architect **Antonio Gaudi**, medieval churches, Roman wall remnants and well-loved promenades and plazas — all produce a distinctive atmosphere. Called "the Paris of Spain" by Hans Christian Andersen for its soulful beauty and its rich cultural heritage, Barcelona has regained some of its youthful glory through recent autonomy and an acceptance of Catalonian culture within Spanish borders.

Barcelona faces the Mediterranean Sea to the southeast, but is said to have "fled from the sea," as its architecture does not focus on its prominent port. The city's plain is bordered by the **Rio Besos**, the **Rio Llobregal** and a semicircle of mountains.

From its beginnings as **Phoenician** and **Carthaginian** trading port, the city grew into a religious center during the **Visigothic** occupation that lasted from the third to the sixth century. After the city passed from the Visigoths to the **Islamic**

Moors in 717 AD, to the **Carolingian Franks** in 801, and to the forces of **al-Mansur of the Umayyad caliphate** in 985, the city's counts consolidated their power and unionized Catalonia and Aragon, reestablishing Barcelona as an excellent trading city.

Barcelona lost some of her power when **Naples** became the capital of the Catalan-Argonese kingdom in 1442, and fell further with the rise of the Ottoman Turks in the Mediterranean. The archduke **Charles III of Austria** was permitted to establish court in Barcelona in 1705, after the **War of the Spanish Succession** put him on the Spanish throne. Barcelona saw a fresh period of economic prosperity when the cotton industry was developed after **Philip V** of Spain captured the city in 1714.

After the **Black Death** in the fourteenth and fifteenth centuries, the repressive governments of Philip V and his successors, and **Napoleon** in the nineteenth century, the city had to cope with twentieth century internal struggles. When the **Spanish Civil War** broke out in 1936, the Catalan Republic surrendered to Spain.

Since the 1970s, when the Catalan language and culture were officially recognized by Spain, Barcelona has regained some of its international importance. In 1980, an autonomous government was established in Catalonia. In 1992, Barcelona hosted the **Olympic Games**, and its charm, as well as that of its nearly 2 million residents, recaptured the world's attention.

An early twentieth century view of the harbor of Barcelona.

Beijing, called **Chi, Yu-chou, Chung-tu, Ta-Tu, Pei-p'ing** ("Northern Peace") and then **Peking** ("Northern Capital"), is home to one of the world's oldest societies. The city has been the capital of **China**, with a few interruptions, for 700 years. It is also the site of some of the earliest known human beings. Fossil remains of **Peking Man** are nearly 500,000 years old.

Although the first capital city built on the site dates back to the **Chou Dynasty** (c. 1111-255 BC), it was the Mongol invasion of China, led by **Genghis Khan** and his successor **Kublai Khan** (1215-94), that established "the Great Capital" of Ta-tu. Bigger than all its predecessors, Ta-tu became China's political center. The Imperial Palace was built, the **T'ung-hui Canal** was dug and the treasures from every corner of the country were collected, astounding the visiting **Marco Polo** in the 1280s.

At the northern apex of the **North China Plain** on the fringe of the **Mongolian Plateau**, Beijing covers approximately 151 square miles (391 square kilometers) and is ruled by an emperor-appointed governor. In the sixteenth century, the central zone was occupied by two walled cities.

The **inner city of Tatar** stood on the original site of the Mongol city of **Ta-Tu**. Within its 15 miles of walls, Tatar City hosted the former **Imperial City**, enclosed by six and a half miles of red plastered walls, and within it, the moated **"Forbidden City"** enclosed the **Emperor's Palaces**, which are now the **Palace Museum**.

The Mongols were overthrown in the fourteenth century. The **Ming Dynasty** was then established, building moats, palaces, temples and new brick walls. In the seventeenth century, the city grew with pavilions and temples outside the city walls, and in the late nineteenth century, the **old Summer Palace** was built and the **new Summer Palace** was completed.

After the revolution of 1912, Peking was made the capital of the Republic of China. When the Japanese invaded China in 1937, the city was occupied by the Japanese troops until 1945, and the capital was relocated to **Chunking**. The Communists under **Mao Zedong** won the **Civil War** that followed **World War II**, and in 1949, the **People's Republic of China** reestablished Peking as China's political and cultural center. The city was a stark and somber place until Mao's death in 1976. China then adopted a free market economy, and Beijing, along with its 5.7 million residents, became more vibrant.

In 1989, the student movement in Beijing launched massive demonstrations, a hunger strike and the occupation of **T'ien-an Men Square**, the city's central plaza. On June 4, government troops brutally massacred thousands. The surviving intellectuals and student leaders went into hiding, hoping to eventually bring about the modernization of their country.

The Temple of Heaven at Beijing.

Beirut, the capital and main port of **Lebanon**, dates back to 3,000 BC, when it was an important port for the Phonecians. Roman colonization first drew attention to Beirut in 14 BC. Located between the hills of **al-Ashrafiyah** and **al-Musaytibah**, Beirut sits in a protected valley, where the Romans built underground aqueducts to nourish the city's growing population. Beirut gained a reputation for its school of law (third through sixth centuries AD), but suffered massive destruction in a rapid series of earthquakes, culminating in the infamous tidal wave of 551 AD. Muslims, who entered Beirut in 635, found mostly ruins and rebuilt the city slowly, feeding a growing commercial port which became the principal port of call in Syria for the Venetian spice merchants.

The **Industrial Revolution** and the Egyptian occupation of Syria in 1832 reinvigorated the declining commercial importance of the city under Ottoman rule. Christian refugees fled to Beirut from civil war in the Syrian mountains, while Protestant missionaries from the United States, Great Britain and Germany further swelled its urban population. At the end of **World War I**, which marked the fall of the Turkish **Ottoman Empire**, the French created the **State of Greater Lebanon**, which became the **Lebanese Republic** in 1926. Beirut evolved as the cosmopolitan hub of economic, social, intellectual and cultural life in the Middle East between 1952 and 1975. A center for tourism, an established leader in banking, and a leading entry port for the area, Beirut's success was cut short by open warfare that erupted between rival Christian and Muslim factions. The **Arab-Israeli War of 1967** brought a stream of Palestinian resistance organizations into Beirut, which gained a reputation as headquarters for the movement. Beirut became a ferocious war zone in the 1980s. Various local militias, as well as Israeli forces and the **Palestinian Liberation Organization (PLO)**, waged vicious warfare in Lebanon, destroying a good deal of **West Beirut** and paralyzing the once vibrant city.

Starting with a population of 100,000 in 1890, the city underwent extreme growth (increasing tenfold between the 1930s and the 1970s) but with the advent of the civil war, it had shrunk to 1.1 million by 1995.

The city of Beirut, before the civil war in Lebanon.

Berlin, the former capital of the **Kingdom of Prussia**, became the capital of the **German Empire** upon its creation in 1871. Ever since then, Berlin has been important to German political history. The city achieved international prominence under **Frederick William the Great Elector** and **Frederick II the Great** in the seventeenth and eighteenth centuries, and exuded a magnetic force in the nineteenth, when East Berlin's **Humboldt University** attracted great minds like **Georg Hegel** and influential theorists like **Karl Marx**. In the same way that Berlin's architecture is punctuated by dazzling buildings and art collections, Berlin's history has been punctuated by intense and fully implemented movements. From the **Revolution of 1848** to **World War I** to the cultural brilliance of the roaring '20s and its cabaret culture, the city's mythological character has shifted and deepened.

From the time that the **National Socialists** (Nazis) came to power in 1933 until the end of **World War II**, Berlin was a focal point of German nationalism — as interpreted by the Nazis. In 1936, Berlin hosted what was billed as "the world's most spectacular Olympic Games," with an underlying agenda of promoting German ethnic superiority. The dark side of the Nazism emerged in the Nazis grisly assault on Germany's Jewish population, eventually leaving millions dead. This siege began in Berlin in 1938 with **Kristallnacht** (Night of Broken Glass), in which Jewish synagogues, businesses and homes were vandalized.

After Germany's defeat in 1945, Germany was divided into four occupation zones by the victorious powers. Berlin's 341 square miles (883 square kilometers), located in the Soviet Zone, were also divided. In 1949, the three western zones became the **Federal Republic of Germany** (West Germany), with **Bonn** as its capital; the Soviet Zone became the **German Democratic Republic** (East Germany), with the eastern part of Berlin as its capital. Attempts by East Berliners to escape communist tyranny in the east compelled the Soviets and East Germans to build the hated **Berlin Wall** in 1961. The physical collapse of the wall in 1989 was symbolic of the collapse of the Communist German Democratic Republic itself.

In 1990, the Federal Republic took over the management of all of Germany and a reunited Berlin, which then had a population of 3.4 million. Berlin became the capital of a reunited Germany, with Bonn remaining the administrative capital.

The city of Berlin: the Breitscheidplatz.
The remains of the Kaiser-Wilhelm-Gedachtnichkirche (Memorial Church) make an interesting contrast to the modern buildings.

As both **Colombia's** capital and its largest city, **Bogotá** is a hospitable and romanticized touchstone for Colombians. Here, the well-loved liberal leader **Jorge Eliecer Gaitan** ruled until his assassination by Republican opponents. Turbulent battles for political power have shattered the peace of this isolated city of 4.8 million citizens, which lies on a fertile plateau in the nation's center. Here, the republican and liberal parties clashed in violent explosions, called **"bogotazo,"** from 1948 to 1958. In spite of these conflicts, Bogotá's leaders have strived to build a "pueblo" that celebrates individualism, mass participation and human grace.

Bogotá is now a city of grand parks and several excellent universities, including the **Universidad de Santo Tomas** (1580) and the **Pontificia Universidad Javeriana** (1622), as well as many other institutions, including the **Botanical Institute, the National Conservatory of Music, the National Museum** and the **Gold Museum**, which houses the world's largest collection of pre-Columbian gold objects. It is also home to the nation's chemical, pharmaceutical and tire industries, as well as the nation's stock exchange and banks.

Located in the naturally fortified Eastern Corillera of the **Andes Mountains**, Colombia's capital has grown slowly from its settlement in 1538, when **Gonzalo Jimenez de Quesada** conquered **Bacata**, the original settlement and main seat of the **Chibcha Indians**. Bogotá became a center for Spanish colonial power in South America once it became the capital city of Nueva Granada. In 1819, the territory gained independence from the Spanish, and Bogotá became the capital city of Gran Colombia, which encompassed Venezuela, Ecuador, Panama and contemporary Colombia. This union dissolved, leaving the city as the capital of the contemporary Republic of Colombia, previously called Nueva Granada.

A detail from an 1850s map of South America, showing New Granada, now Colombia.

19

Commercially, if not politically or geographically, **Bombay** is the center of **India**. Bordered by the **Arabian Sea** to the west and **Bombay Harbor** to the east, the island has existed as the chief western seaport since the mid-eighteenth century. Before the **United States Civil War** stopped the export of cotton from the southern states, Bombay was the world's chief cotton market. The export of Indian textiles, leather, steel, cement and oil created fortunes for a few families in the industrial center, but left much of the current population impoverished. Thousands of Bombay's citizens sleep and live in its streets.

Nestled in a low-lying plain that is sheltered by bordering hills, the city covers 95 square miles (246 square kilometers). Several bridges link it to India's mainland. Bombay's narrow streets are crowded with beggars and businessmen, the latter working in the Indian stock exchange and banks. The primarily **Hindu** population (up to 12.9 million from 822,000 in 1890) is split, not on issues of religion or race, but of language. In response to these tensions, Bombay was divided into two states, **Maharashta** and **Gujaret.**

Even though Bombay's tourism has flourished, increasing by 400 percent since the British granted India independence in August of 1947, the city suffers extreme unemployment. Great poverty exists on the same streets where great opulence in architecture and adornment are common, mainly because ninety percent of the money invested in India's industrial complex belongs to government. Along with its industrialized mechanism, Bombay has created a second booming business: film. Like the Hollywood of the 1930s, Bombay raises its film stars to inhuman heights. This industry, along with the climate of the **University of Bombay** (1857), is speaking to and influencing the city's increasingly Westernized youth. There are signs that the young Indian population recognizes its powerful majority in Bombay and may exert pressure on the static government to change the impoverished state of its people.

An early twentieth century street scene in Bombay.

Boston, capital of **Massachusetts** and home to 574,000 people, retains the flavor and mood of its important position in colonial, pre-1776 America. Holding onto its history, which began its foundation with Puritan Englishmen seeking religious freedom from the **Church of England**, Boston's colonial architecture grandly refers to the city's early vitality. Eighteenth century Boston was an important center of the growing opposition to English rule, with the storming and gutting of the governor's house in response to the **Stamp Act** (1765), the **Boston Massacre** (1770), in which British troops fired on civilians, and the **Boston Tea Party** (1773), in which British tea valued at over £9,000 pounds was dropped into **Boston Harbor**.

After the American **War of Independence**, early nineteenth century Boston drew great men, who established textile mills. During this time, Bostonians popularized the **Unitarian doctrine**, which eventually splintered the Catholic and Protestant churches. Boston's citizens also witnessed the move towards **Transcendentalism**, which colored the century's art and thought, and they supported the first outspoken anti-slavery liberals like **William Lloyd Garrison** (1805-1879).

Physically, the city is divided into its north and south ends by **Town Cove**, which juts in from the harbor on the east. So much land has been reclaimed (the city now covers 50 square miles, 129 square kilometers), that the peninsula is now indistinguishable from the rest of the mainland. The city's position on the **Shawmut Peninsula**, almost completely surrounded by water, led to many wharves and shipyards being erected. Boston's early financial success built many of the nation's oldest and finest buildings, designed by architects like **Charles Bulfinch**. Many of these landmarks have been destroyed in favor of modern apartments and offices, but the **Old Corner Book Store** (1711) still exists, as does the **Old State House** (1711), which was the colonial town's original center.

Boston has also developed a great many universities, libraries and museums. As well as the world-renowned **Harvard University** in nearby Cambridge, the city has **Boston University** (1869), **Northeastern University** (1898), and **Suffolk University** (1906). The **Boston Symphony Orchestra**, founded in 1881, performs at **Symphony Hall**.

Faneuil Hall, Boston, where the revolutionary meetings were held.

As well as being the capital city of **Belgium**, Brussels (**Bruxelles** in French, **Brussel** in Flemish) also headquarters the **European Communities**, which include the **European Economic Community, the European Coal & Steel Community** and the **North Atlantic Treaty Organization (NATO)**. Belgian King Leopold II said, "Brussels can become the turntable of Europe," referring to its proximity to all of Europe's major cities and its growing popularity with European congresses and international travellers. Brussels courts its visitors with its central square, the **Grand Place**, on the same site as its original medieval marketplace.

Born as a petite fortified castle on a small island in the **Senne River**, Brussels grew past its heart shaped walls and into one of the major towns of the Duchy of **Brabant**. It gained an international reputation for the production of fine fabrics, which were favorites of Parisian and Venetian designers during the thirteenth and fourteenth centuries. Brussels has some of the finest Gothic spires and baroque flourishes in Europe. The city's face, including its Town Hall (built between 1402-1454), was formed mainly during the **Burgundian period** (1430-1477). In the sixteenth century, Brussels suffered the viciousness of the **Protestant Reformation** and the growth of the **Counter-Reformation**. The reign of **Archduke Albert** and **Isabella** (1598-1633) helped in the construction of many of the city's baroque churches, but the late seventeenth century brought repeated invasions by **Louis XIV** of France, who left hundreds of Brussels' buildings in flames. The **Brabant Revolt** (1788-90) against **Joseph II of Austria** brought the French in again, and the Belgian principalities were annexed to France during the **Napoleonic era**. Belgium won its independence from the **Kingdom of the Netherlands** in 1830, and Brussels was named the capital.

The Germans occupied Brussels for the four years of **World War I** (1914-1918), and the **National Committee for Relief and Food** was headquartered in Brussels to fend off the abuses of the German forces. The city was occupied again during **World War II**, suffering little damage and attempting to appease the Germans by appointing Flemish nationalist **Jan Grauls** to head the governing council. Britain freed Belgium in 1944, and Brussels was chosen to host the **World's Fair** in 1958.

The city has weathered international conflict and rivalry between Belgium's Flemish and French nationalists. Brussels' 990,000 citizens live in the only officially bilingual city in the country.

St. Gudale, Brussels.

Budapest, the capital city of **Hungary**, was actually two cities, **Buda** and **Pest**, until they were unified in 1872. Buda grew on the river terraces of the western banks of the **Danube River**, and Pest, on the flat plains of the eastern bank. As Europe's second largest city, it covers 203 square miles (525 square kilometers) and is connected over the beautiful Danube by bridges. Particularly during the nineteenth century, Budapest's two million residents have grown fat off Western investment, robust private enterprise and a tolerated black market.

Along with its cobbled streets, gothic homes and Buda's three green hilltops and bridges, the city preserves the works of Hungary's best artists and composers. **Ferenc Erkel** and **Erno Dohnanyi** are among them, while another, **Franz Liszt**, established a music academy in 1875.

Among the city's finest architectural works are the **Royal Palace**, restored on top of Buda's **Castle Hill**, the **National Library, the Historical Museum of Budapest** and the **Hungarian National Gallery**, all housed in the restored baroque palace complex built for **Maria Theresa, Queen of Hungary** (1740-1780). The Inner Town of Pest remains intact, though not much remains from the original town walls.

Buda not only protected its own people, but people from other towns. When Pest was sacked by the **Mongols** in 1241, **Bela IV** allowed its citizens to settle within Buda's fortified castle walls. After the death of **Matthias I** in 1490, however, Buda's security was gone. The Turks came in and held the city from 1541 until 1686, when it was liberated by the **Holy Roman Emperor Leopold I**. By 1703, both Buda and Pest were recognized as royal free towns. In 1783, Buda became Hungary's administrative center, the **High Court** moving there, while the university was transferred to Pest. Under the **Hapsburg monarchy**, Buda maintained its aristocracy, but Pest took up the nationalist cause, leading to two distinct characters.

The early twentieth century was devastating for Budapest. A working class movement emerged before **World War I**, and the disintegration of **Austria-Hungary** in 1918 made it possible for the radical **Socialist National Council** to take control. The next year, the Communists seized power for four months. Before order could finally be restored, Rumanian troops sacked the city. In 1920, Budapest became the capital of independent Hungary, which allied itself with Germany in **World War II**, only to become occupied by Soviet Forces in 1944. The latter installed a Communist regime, which Budapest's people rebelled against in 1956. The brutality with which the Soviets crushed the rebellion put Budapest at the center of the darkest moment of the Soviets' half century of Eastern European domination.

In the 1980s, Hungary became one of Eastern Europe's first nations to begin dismantling its Communist economy, and again asserted its democratic will in a move toward multiparty politics.

The Hungarian Parliament, Budapest.

Buenos Aires, named for the patron saint **St. Mary of the Good Air** and home to the world's widest boulevard, is the bustling capital of **Argentina**, known as "the Paris of South America" for its elegance.

Buenos Aires was founded twice on the flat plain known as **the Pampa**, where the **Parana River delta** widens to meet the **Rio de la Plata**. The center of the city sits on a bluff that overlooks the river, while the rest of the city lies on flat floodplains that are bordered by other small rivers. With a metropolitan area of 77 square miles (200 square kilometers), the city centers on the Federal District. It contains less than one third of the metropolitan area's population and is surrounded by suburbs, including the vast shanty towns of corrugated metal shacks, which make up 40 percent of the metropolis' homes and house thirty percent of the population.

Buenos Aires' exciting history is laced with political unrest and qualified by risky individualism. Its first foundation in 1536 was sacked by Indians and not resettled until 1580. With a good port — now the largest in South America — Buenos Aires traded with the British, exporting thousands of tons of cereals, cattle hides and dry beef to Brazil and the Caribbean Islands. By the middle of the eighteenth century, Buenos Aires was thriving, and the **Bourbon monarchy** named it the capital of the Rio de la Plata, in hopes of increasing taxes and sheltering the city from competitors, especially the British. The elite were split into two factions: one that traded internationally with Cuba and Brazil, and the regionally-based group governed by the viceroyalty that was recognized by the Crown.

In 1806 and 1807, when the local militia fought off British troops and **Napoleon** put his brother **Joseph Bonaparte** on the Spanish throne, Buenos Aires was the first province to declare independence, severing its ties with Spanish rule. In 1816, the rest of the provinces capitulated, and Buenos Aires was named capital of the United Provinces of Rio de la Plata.

One of the most populous cities in the world (three million in 1990), as well as the financial and cultural center of the nation, Buenos Aires suffers some of the worst problems plaguing big cities: increasing pollution, urban congestion, inadequate public services, limited land area for continuing expansion, and a lack of jobs for unskilled immigrants, who swell the poor population of Buenos Aires' outlying shanty towns. Along with its stretched resources and urbanized poor, Buenos Aires has a class of wealthy, highly literate people who are responsible for the artist colony of **La Boca**, the **Nobel Prize winning scientists** from the **University of Buenos Aires**, the parks, plazas and tree-lined boulevards that ring the city and the enduring pride of the metropolitan populace. Symbolized by the **tango**, the passionate dance which originated in Buenos Aires, the people of this region remain loyal to their city and romantically engaged by their temperate, lush surroundings.

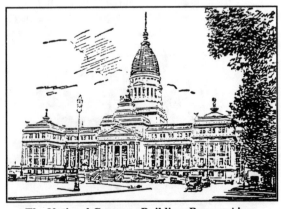

The National Congress Building, Buenos Aires.

Cairo, the capital and undisputed jewel of **Egypt**, is Africa's largest city. Sitting mainly on the east bank of the **Nile River**, it has dominated modern Egypt's cultural and economic wealth. Elements of ancient, historical architecture are mixed with elegant, high-rise apartment buildings and hotels, which are graced with rooms overlooking the lush vegetation of the Nile's riverbanks. Sitting in the shadows of the great pyramids at Giza, the only surviving monuments of the seven wonders of the ancient world, Cairo lies next to Memphis, whose history, along with that of Giza, reaches back 5,000 years.

The city has been called "fan-shaped," being narrow in the south, where the desert sands encroach, and wider in the north, where the land grows more fertile with the Nile Delta. Cairo's walled core, featuring major bazaars as well as markets for gold, textiles, spices, amber and leather, is one of its three most heavily populated and oldest areas. Along with **Bulaq** to the northwest and **Misr al-Oadimah** to the south, the city's core borders the Parisian-styled, modern city, which sits directly on the Nile's eastern bank. In contrast to the modern city, narrow streets, domed mosques, four-storied fired brick homes, fountained courtyards between separate dwellings for men and women, and decadent wooden ornaments characterize the old districts. Farther to the east, the foothills of the **Arabian Desert** and **Red Mountain's** petrified forest are wonders of the Egyptian landscape.

South of contemporary Cairo lies "**the City of the Dead**," where exquisite shrines and mausoleums stand in honor of early religious leaders. North from the City of the Dead, the southern quarter of contemporary Cairo, called **Misr al-Oadimah (Old Cairo)**, sits on the site of the Roman walled city, where the **Coptic churches** still stand.

Medieval Cairo reached its zenith in the thirteenth century under **Mamluk**. As a gateway to the East-West spice trade and the capital of the empire that ruled Egypt until 1516, the city received much tribute, and its population swelled to 500,000 people by 1340.

It was the Black Death of 1348 that decimated the population. The spice trade monopoly was broken by **Vasco da Gama's** voyage to India from Portugal, and the Turks succeeded in turning Cairo into a provincial capital after their victory of 1517. **Muhammad Ali** founded the dynasty that ruled Egypt from 1805 to 1952. The twentieth century has seen enormous population growth (from 375,000 in 1890 to 6.5 million in 1990), though the city's area remains at 104 square miles (269 square kilometers). Excellent universities, like **Cairo University**, **Ain Shams University** and **al-Azhar University**, attract students from all over Egypt. The city has founded numerous museums, such as **the Egyptian Museum** on the famous **Tahrir Square**, where the riches of **Tutankhamen** (1400 BC) are displayed.

The Citadel in Cairo.

Calcutta was once the capital of **British India** (1772-1912) and is the current capital of the Indian state of **West Bengal**. Its name was taken from **Kali**, the black goddess of destruction, when it was founded by the East India Company's **Job Charnock**, who in 1690 moved his factory from the city of **Hooghly** to Calcutta's site on the **Ganges River**. Calcutta now produces forty percent of all India's wealth, but its lower class' poverty, among the world's worst, has led to a proliferation of slums, inhabited by one third of Calcutta's 9,914,000 people. Though the poverty is atrocious, Calcutta retains an intellectual excitement and an artistic drive that colors its society and physicality. Art exhibits, book fairs and musical concerts draw huge crowds, making Calcutta a cultural oasis for **India**. The city's people live in the most cosmopolitan of ancient societies, debating politics and art with frenzied passion and launching fabulous productions of Sarte and Becket.

Journalist **Sasthi Brata** describes the city's extremities as they appear side by side: "Narrow gullies, rat-infested lanes, open sewers, maimed beggars, grandly staircased clubs, acres of billiard-table lawns, manicured and bordered with marigolds, bougainvillaeas, rhododendrons, and gladioli, comprise a canvas made from the woof and warp of history...."

Calcutta's history is deeply tied to British history. As an original site for the **British East India Company**, the city originated under an agreement that the British would be granted freedom of trade for the price of 3,000 rupees a year. With the **Maratha** invasion in 1742, the British received permission to build a moat around the city's area, but by 1772, when **Warren Hastings** made Calcutta the British Indian capital, the British city had been won in war.

The capital was moved to **Delhi** in 1912, and the city continued to decline as it had since the Indian viceroy partitioned **Bengal** in 1905, even though the partition was annulled. Social conditions became desperate with overcrowding, and riots broke out in 1926, as Indians demanded home rule. **Mahatma Gandhi** preached noncompliance and the riots intensified in 1930.

In 1946, the partition of British India was imminent and tensions rose between the city's **Muslim** and **Hindu** populations. The Partition of Bengal in 1947 severed East Bengal (East Pakistan until 1971, independent **Bangladesh** thereafter) from West and left Calcutta as the capital of West Bengal only. The city lost a portion of its valuable trade, but immigrants continued to flock to its overcrowded streets. From 1890 to 1990, the population rose from 978,000 to 11 million.

A temple and park in Calcutta, circa 1920.

Canton (Kuang-chou), southern **China's** largest city and the capital of **Kwangtung Province**, was the world's largest city at the beginning of the nineteenth century. Its highly educated populace was always politically active, becoming involved in the **Canton Uprising of 1911**, which led to the **Chinese Revolution** against the **Manchu Dynasty**.

Canton sits mainly on the north bank of the Pearl River. The **Yueh-hsiu district**, on the site of the old city, remains the commercial center and government seat. As in older days, winding, crowded streets and traditional-style housing can still be found, but skyscrapers, numerous parks and wide, modern avenues now dominate. Among the district's excellent monuments are the **Canton Municipal Museum**, housed in a red pagoda from 1380, the **Peasant Movement Institute**, located near the city's center, and the **Huai-sheng Mosque** (627), considered the oldest in China.

Also amassed in the city's center are most of Canton's 3 million residents, who speak the Chinese dialect known as Cantonese. Their annual **Spring Festival** highlights an incomparable flower show, the city's museums are always full, and numerous colleges and universities flourish, including **Sun Yat-sen University, Chinan University, Canton College of Traditional Chinese Medicine** and **Canton Institute of Mechanical Engineering**.

The city grew rich under the original Chinese regimes, adding Buddhist temples and developing a community maintained by Arab and Hindu traders. The city's walls were enlarged to handle growth during the **Sung Dynasty** (960-1279), and many Chinese families flocked south to avoid the **Mongol invasion** of northern China in the thirteenth and fourteenth centuries. The **Manchu Dynasty** ruled from 1644 to 1911, and Canton was made the capital of the Viceroyalty of Kwangtung and Kwangsi. The **British East India Company** began trading operations in 1699, and the **First Opium War** (1839-1842) erupted when the Cantonese seized and destroyed huge amounts of illegal opium brought in by the British, who encouraged its use in order to subdue Indian and Chinese workers. It took a ransom of $6 million to save Canton from being destroyed after China's massive defeat.

The **Second Opium War** broke out between Britain, France and China in 1856, and Canton was occupied by Anglo-French forces until 1861. At the same time, a growing anti-dynastic fervor produced the **Taiping Rebellion** (1820-1864). The movement went underground after its first defeat to perfect its ideals, but then rose to the surface again with the dynamic Sun Yat-sen in 1885.

In 1949, after Japanese occupation in **World War II**, the Communist government took control and the city's growth continued despite periods of constant strife, including the **Cultural Revolution** of 1966-1967. Having emerged as one of the most populated cities in modern China, Canton has also become an important commercial center, characterized by a growing Westernization and a new regard for capitalism.

The Si River at Canton in the early 1900s.

Cape Town was founded north of the **Cape of Good Hope** on the site of the **Dutch East India Company**'s small resting station for ships pulling into **Table Bay**. Since then, it has become the legislative capital for the **Republic of South Africa** and the capital of **Cape Province**. Because of its history as the first European settlement in South Africa, it has been called "the mother city." Cape Town sits amidst mountains and sea on one of the nation's most beautiful locations. Parts of the city encircle the steep slopes of Table Mountain, its neighboring peaks and Table Bay's lovely shores. Other parts nestle on the flats below the slopes and stretch south to False Bay. Originally only a small settlement between Table Bay and Table Mountain, the city has grown to a 116 square mile area (300 square kilometers) with a populace numbering over 1.9 million.

From the beginning, the shore ran parallel to the city's main streets. On them, old buildings, like the **Castle of Good Hope**, built between 1666 and 1679 by the Dutch East India Company, still stand. The nearby **Botanic Gardens** are overshadowed by early government buildings, and much of the surviving early architecture reflects traditional Netherlands styles, including flat roofs, projecting porches and distinctive gables.

With the institution of official racial "apartheid" (separation of races) in the 1940s, black residents of Cape Town were restricted to either **Guguletu** and **Nyanga West** within the city, or the two settlements outside the city limits. Blacks began to move into the city in great numbers during the 1980s, leading to the government establishment of the township **Khayelitsha**, east of Mitchells Plain. To move people towards this new area, the overcrowded squatter camps, organically sprung up to house new arrivals, were destroyed in 1986.

In 1993, South Africa abolished apartheid and elected a black leader, **Nelson Mandela**. Today, all of Cape Town's citizens — black, white and mixed-race — share the city's excellent cultural highlights. Though universities traditionally accepted students regardless of race and based only on merit, other centers, like the **South African Cultural History Museum** and the **Cape Town Symphony Orchestra,** are now legally bound to ignore race for the first time.

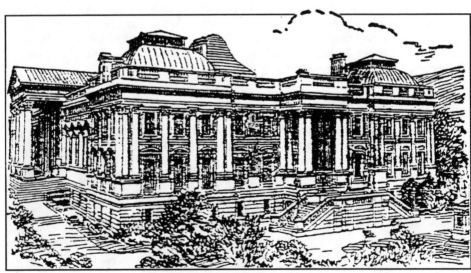

The Houses of Parliament in Cape Town.

Caracas is Venezuela's capital as well as its great cultural, industrial and commercial center. The city owes much of its current prosperity to petroleum, which ushered in a new age in 1936, the year of dictator **Juan Vicente Gomez**'s death. Although President **Antonio Guzman Blanco** tried to make Caracas into a mirror of Paris in 1783, it wasn't until the last half of the twentieth century, when Caracas began drawing government and private investments, that the city expanded to 1.3 million residents (almost twice that of the nation's fourth largest city). Under the dictatorship of **Marcos Perez Jimenez** (1951-1957), slums were razed, replaced by brightly painted, high-rise apartments and a maze of superhighways sprang up, highlighting an age of great expansion within Caracas' limited 54-square-mile (140 square kilometers) area.

Established by **Juan Rodriguez Suarez** in 1561, Caracas was founded on the northern-most hills of the **Andes Mountains** on Venezuela's northern coast. Indian attacks destroyed the original town, and in 1566 **Diego de Losada** resettled the district, founding the city of Santiago de Leon de Caracas, named after the apostle James, the patron saint of Spain, and **Ponce de Leon**, the provincial governor. The city was laid out in a rectangle of twenty-four squares surrounding a public plaza, with the city's streets set in cobbled straight lines.

Brick houses, featuring straw roofs, patios, decadent arcades and slave quarters, were fashionable among the small class of wealthy landowners, who occupied the city's eastern margins and the Caribbean coast. The middle class emerged in the city's core, where fine colonial buildings still stand, and Caracas' laborers still live in western and southern hillside shanty towns.

In 1577, after Caracas acquired its status as a provincial capital, it was sacked by **English buccaneers** in 1595. Two earthquakes decimated the original Spanish architecture in 1755 and 1812, and smallpox decimated the Indian population which formed the main resistance to settlement.

In 1783, the great **Simon Bolivar** was born in Caracas to a prominent family. After being schooled in political affairs, he went on to liberate Venezuela from Spanish rule in 1830.

A magnificent view of Caracas and Avila Mountain.

Casablanca, meaning "white house," was founded by Spanish merchants in the sixteenth century on the site of a small twelfth century village called **Anfa**, which served as a pirate port for thieves who attacked passing ships from **Morocco's** northern coast. Nothing is left of the original pirate town, destroyed by the **Portuguese** in 1468. It wasn't until their return, in 1515, that Casa Branca, or Casablanca, was employed as an important trade port.

After the devastating **earthquake of 1755**, the **Alawi sultan** had to rebuild the city again. French settlers moved in quickly, becoming the population's majority around 1907. They rebuilt the harbor as Morocco's chief port, spurring the rapid commercial progress that swelled the city's population to 3.5 million by 1990, compared to 10,000 residents in 1890.

In 1943, during **World War II**, US President Franklin D. Roosevelt and British Prime Minister Winston Churchill met in Casablanca to plan the strategies that eventually led to the Germany's defeat.

The city's central core, with its narrow streets and whitewashed brick and stone faced homes, is still partly enclosed by the original city walls. Beyond the walls is the old French quarter, spreading to 35 square miles (90 square kilometers), which is Morocco's economic and business capital, served by Casablanca's busy port. Housing the city's luxury hotels and banks, more than half the nation's bank transactions and industrial production take place here.

This section also contains Casablanca's administrative center, based in **United Nations Square** and **Muhammad V Square**. Bordering this area near the coast are the villas and gardens of the residential sections. On the outskirts, shanty towns house the poorer Arab population.

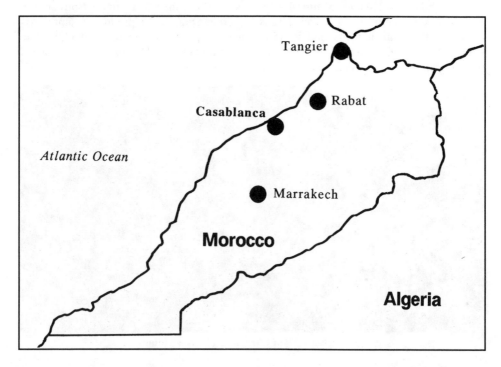

Chicago is famous for its stock yards and sprawling industrial area, its invaluable port on the Great Lakes, its position as North America's most important railroad hub, and its enduring spirit during the Great Chicago Fire of 1871. It is distinguished by its historical literary citizens, including **Saul Bellow, Gwendolyn Brooks, Carl Sandburg** and **Theodore Dreiser**, and its world class architecture by masters like **Frank Lloyd Wright**.

Chicago's current size — equaling 762 square miles (1,973 square kilometers) — grew out of the trading post established here by **John Kinzie** in 1796.

The steel-frame skyscraper originated in Chicago. In 1885, the **Home Insurance Building** was completed, and in the next nine years, 21 buildings were built, ranging from 12 to 16 stories high. Growing to prominence in the nineteenth century because of its location and its importance as a transportation hub, Chicago hosted the **World's Columbian Exposition** in 1893, outbidding even New York and Washington DC.

During the Prohibition Era of the 1920s, Chicago became infamous for its organized crime bosses, including **Al Capone**, who exerted control over business and sometimes politics. Warring mobsters were prone to great violence, and Chicago's populace watched carefully as viciousness grew, culminating in events like the **St. Valentine's Day Massacre** of 1929. At the same time, the city was alive with music and color, hidden in the private **speakeasies** where **flappers** danced and money fell through the hands like water.

Chicago was also the home base for some of America's most inventive theater troupes, including **Second City**, and the **Art Institute of Chicago** is considered one of the nation's best art schools.

The city's mayors have attracted national interest, especially **Richard J. Daley**, who ruled Chicago politics for many decades until his death in 1976, and his son and namesake, who came to power a decade later.

Today Chicago is the favorite American city for conventions. It has grown into the most important rail hub for Illinois Central, Burlington Northern and the Atchison Topeka & Santa Fe. The latter two merged operations in 1995 to become the largest rail system in the Western Hemisphere. Chicago, as the heart of the nation's railroads, is their centerpiece. The city's lovely lakefront is nationally known for its rich and beautiful homes, parks and beaches, and Chicago's 2.8 million residents are still considered some of the most wild and inventive people in America.

A 1940s view of the city skyline, looking north from the Chicago Board of Trade Building.

Copenhagen, the romantic capital of Denmark, has balanced the green copper roofs and renaissance buildings built in the 1400s under **King Christian IV** with today's modern amusements, including the **Tivoli Gardens** with their shooting galleries, classical symphony and pantomime ballets. Called "the Paris of Scandinavia" by some of its 1.3 million residents, Copenhagen fascinates visitors with its palaces, its crooked, old world shopping streets, its stock exchange building, which is the world's oldest and adorned with a dragon tail spire, its observatory, which is enhanced with a statue of Danish astronomer **Tycho Brahe**, and its museums, including the **National Museum,** which was once the **Prinsens Palace**, and the **Palace of Rosenborg,** which is now the museum of the royal family.

Archbishop Absalon, who freed Denmark from the **Wendish pirates**, is credited with its founding since he built a castle (now rebuilt as **Christiansborg Palace**) on an inlet that was fortified with ramparts and a moat in 1167 and made the capital of Denmark in 1445. The town continued to grow up around it, suffering much damage during the civil and religious conflicts of the **Protestant Reformation,** and suffering further conflict during the **wars with Sweden** (1658-1660) and the **British bombardment** of the early 1800s. But, unlike many of Europe's treasured cities, Copenhagen suffered no damage during **World War II**, as Denmark was taken with almost no resistance.

Copenhagen has always thrived on trade and shipping, and has recently added industry, focusing on shipbuilding, machinery production, canning and brewing. It was in Copenhagen that **Emil Christian Hansen** bred the first pure lager yeast for the brewing of Danish beer.

Copenhagen also developed a number of excellent schools, including the **University of Copenhagen** (1479), which has a **Botanical Garden** with 15,000 species, the **Technical University of Denmark** (1829), the **Royal Academy of Music** (1867), the **Royal Veterinary and Agricultural College** (1856), the **Copenhagen School of Economics and Business Administration** (1917) and the **Engineering Academy of Denmark** (1957).

The city's heart is kept within **Town Hall Square**, connected to the city's former center, **King's New Square**, by an old street of shops. Laid out in the seventeenth century, King's New Square still holds the **French Embassy in Thott Palace**, the **Royal Academy of Fine Arts in Charlottenborg Palace**, as well as the **Royal Theatre** (1874).

The harbor at Copenhagen.

Damascus, located in the orchards of the **Al-Ghutah Oasis** and once called "the Pearl of the East," is the capital of **Syria**. Historians have suggested that the city was founded even before written history, and it is believed to be the world's oldest continually inhabited city. As the capital of the ancient Umayyad Caliphate of Greater Syria, it ruled over a vast empire in the eighth century. The **Great Mosque of Damascus** was begun in 705, and the current **citadel** was rebuilt in 1219. Some of the **Old City**'s houses are still patioed and adorned with outdoor water fountains, although this architectural fashion has died away and is no longer reproduced. The original **Damascus steel** sword blades, famous in India and described by **Aristotle** as early as 334 BC, are also not made anymore. However, the markets continue to feature Damascus' fine mosaics, silk brocades and carved woodwork.

In the sixteenth century, when the Turks had conquered the Middle East and established the **Ottoman Empire**, Damascus gained its enduring reputation as a spiritually important city to the many Muslim pilgrims, who passed through on their way to **Mecca**. The Turks moved their marketplace north to the city of **Aleppo**, and a rivalry developed between the two.

After **World War I**, **Greater Syria** was divided into six autonomous areas under French rule. Damascus became a tightly controlled province inhabited by well-educated Arab nationalists. The **People's Party** was formed to re-unify Syria and combat the French repression of newspapers and civil liberties. In 1925, the Aleppo and Damascus provinces were united.

Today, Damascus is a modern city of 1.4 million where the religious and artistic riches of its ancient existence are clearly evident. Located at the base of the **Qasiyun Mountain** in an oasis fed by the **Barada River** and bordered by open plains, the city encompasses an area of 41 square miles (105 square kilometers). Fruits, olives and grapes grow in the irrigated lands outside the old city, where the principal mosques and markets are located.

An antique engraving of the Mosque of Omar in Damascus.

New Delhi, the modern capital of **India**, is situated immediately south of the city of **Delhi**, now called **Old Delhi**. Both cities have seen so much growth since achieving independence that they have melded into a greater Delhi. Old Delhi's many monuments are excellent examples of **Indo-Muslim** architecture, **Pashtun style** architecture (1193-1320), which features fine domes and tiles, and **Mughal styles**, which use elaborate surfaces and marble, as evidenced in the **Principal Mosque**. The crumbling ruins of 400-year-old forts can be seen in many places unattended and unrespected.

Old Delhi on its current site was built by **Shah Jahan** in 1638, who ruled from his famous Peacock throne of emeralds, diamonds and rubies. Delhi was then the capital of a succession of empires, including the **Mui'izzi Dynasty** in the thirteenth century, the **Mughal Empire**, under **Babur**, in the sixteenth, and the **Persian Empire** in the eighteenth. Persians took the empire's prized 109 carat **Koh-i-noor diamond**, which was later presented to **Queen Victoria** by the **East India Company** in 1850. Of the many emperors who have ruled from Delhi, seven have rebuilt the city on nearby sites. Historians report that Delhi's smaller settlements number 15. New Delhi, designed by **Sir Edwin Lutyens**, was built as the capital of **British India** in 1912.

Once confined to the West Bank of the **Yamuna River**, a tributary of the **Ganges**, Delhi has grown to 138 square miles (357 square kilometers) and encompasses the city of New Delhi, the sites of former Delhis and the eastern bank of the river. The population had exploded to nine million by 1990, up from 193,000 in 1890. The boom has led to the overcrowding and poverty problems that are endemic in India's major cities.

London journalist **Sasthi Brata** calls New Delhi "arguably the most beautifully designed and grandly conceived capital in the world. Radially set out, with fountains in the middle of every roundabout, the wide avenues branch out from the central hubs. The Presidential Palace (where the British viceroys used to live) is built out of red sandstone and is the most majestic building of its kind I have ever seen, including Buckingham Palace and the Palais de l'Elysee."

The Mosque of Shah Jehan in Delhi in the early twentieth century.

28. DETROIT, USA
Founded in 1701

Located on the **Detroit River**, opposite Windsor, Ontario in Canada, the city of **Detroit** grew from a small trading post to a modern industrial city of one million which, since the beginning of the twentieth century, has seen its fortunes tied to the ups and downs of the American automobile industry.

Founded by a French trader in 1701, who built the city into an important fur-trading post, Detroit remained a French city until its surrender to the British during the **French & Indian War**. The city became the capital of the newly created **Michigan Territory** in 1805. The **War of 1812** put Detroit under British control again, but the Americans recaptured it in 1813.

Detroit grew swiftly after it became a center for the processing of water, grain and other agricultural products being shipped to Europe and the rest of America. From 1837 to 1847, Detroit was the capital of **Michigan,** and after the **Civil War** (1861-1865), the city grew into an industrial powerhouse, encompassing an area of 468 square miles (1,212 square kilometers).

Henry Ford, designer of the **Model T**, helped Detroit gain its position as the au-

The 1995 Oldsmobile Aurora is symbolic of Detroit's role as "Motor City".

tomobile capital of the world. **World War I** moved the city into the lucrative business of military armaments production. Sensitive to the rise and fall of the nation's industrial needs, Detroit has felt the undulations of the nation's economy more than most other cities.

Culturally, Detroit remains a rich city, even during the civil disturbances of the late twentieth century. Along with the **Detroit Symphony Orchestra**, the **Detroit Institute of Arts**, the **Cranbrook Academy of Art** and the **Henry Ford Museum**, the city is home to Motown Records (short for "Motor Town"), where musical superstars, like the Supremes, made their gold records, revolutionizing the sounds of pop music.

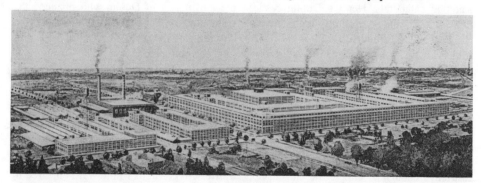

Detroit has been the world capital of auto manufacturing since the early twentieth century.

Dublin's site on the **River Liffey** has been inhabited since prehistoric times. Dublin was first settled by the Celts, who were attacked in the ninth century by **Vikings** from the north. After burning Celtic monasteries and plundering the wealth of the Irish Christian churches, the Vikings stayed in 841 for their first winter in the county of Dublin, where they settled permanently, adopting the Irish name for "dark pool."

In 1167, the Norse exiled the **king of Leinster**, who had claimed the high kingship of **Ireland**. He later returned from exile with a Welsh army to retake the city. Afraid this army would claim Ireland, **King Henry II** sent an army of his own, making Dublin the Irish capital in 1172 and imposing English rule from **Dublin Castle**. Though enriched by the wealth of Henry II, Dublin grew slowly, until in 1685 thousands of French immigrant weavers came after the **Edict of Nantes** was revoked. Protestant Dublin flourished after **Flemish weavers** followed the French, and Dublin's textiles began attracting English attention. English lords and masters came and built their lavish townhouses around the two standing cathedrals, Henry's Dublin castle, built in 1212, and archbishop John Comyn's **St. Patrick's Cathedral**, built in 1181. A Protestant parliament enforced laws limiting land ownership and wealth to those of the Protestant faith, leaving the Irish Catholic population impoverished and indebted to their English lords.

In 1801, the **Act of Union** abolished the **Irish Parliament**, and the city began to decline from its cultural peak. **Penal Laws** were restrictive enough to cripple the citizenship, until a Roman Catholic middle class began to emerge in the mid-nineteenth century. In 1841, the city's first Roman Catholic mayor since the seventeenth century was elected, and in 1854, the **Catholic University of Ireland** was founded.

By the twentieth century, all of Ireland's populace was starving for home rule. Dublin became the focal point of the unrest that led to the 1916 **Easter Rising**, a milestone on the bloody road to eventual independence from Britain. The British retaliated with great force, capturing and executing fifteen rebel leaders, who immediately became heroes to their countrymen. Passage of the **Irish Free State Act of 1922** allowed for the creation of an independent dominion with the British Commonwealth. The Irish Free State, which included 26 of Ireland's 32 counties, took Dublin as its capital and became a republic in 1949, severing all ties with Britain. The six counties of Northern Ireland, meanwhile, remained part of the United Kingdom.

From the **Celts** of pre-history to the contemporary Irish men and women, numbering 866,000, Dublin has always been the cultural heart of Ireland. As the headquarters for brewing magnate **Sir Benjamin Lee Guinness**, the lord mayor of Dublin who financed the restoration of **St. Patrick's Cathedral**, the city remains the perfect center for Irish religion and commerce.

Dublin, which is home to **Trinity College**, has always been regarded as an important literary center, nurturing some of the greatest writers of the past two centuries, including **Jona-than Swift, William Congreve, Oscar Wilde, Samuel Beckett, William Butler Yeats** and the beloved **James Joyce**, all of whom were nurtured in the depth of Irish spirit.

Once, the medieval city of **Edinburgh**, like medieval London, was surrounded by a great wall. It is bordered by two castles: the **Palace of Holyrood House**, the official royal residence, and **Edinburgh Castle**. Between these, the city grew, enduring the tragic English battle for domination over Scottish royalty, hailing **Mary, Queen of Scots** and weathering attacks by **Henry the VIII** after she failed to wed his son **Edward**. By the late eighteenth century, the city had grown from one of merchants and craftspeople to a royal capital, inspired by the **Victorian enlightenment**.

In trying to assess a native love for the windy, bitterly cold city, **Robert Louis Stevenson** said, "Beautiful as she is, she is not so much beautiful as interesting. She is preeminently **Gothic**, and all the more so since she has set herself off with some Greek airs, and erected classic temples on her crags. In a word, and above all, she is a curiosity...."

Along with Stevenson, great Western thinkers like **Sir Walter Scott** were trained in Edinburgh, the great legal and medical center of Britain. The tradition, the same as

Mary, Queen of Scots.

the one that educated such scholars as philosopher **David Hume** and physicist **William Cullen**, has developed Edinburgh's reputation as a city of literati and of great social grace; the best mix of British and Scottish intellect.

Encompassing 101 square miles (261 square kilometers), Edinburgh supports a population of 440,000, which is roughly twice its population of at the end of the nineteenth century.

An early twentieth century view of Edinburgh.

Florence was one of the most glorious cities of Medieval and Renaissance **Italy**. Home to the great fourteenth century poet, **Dante Alighieri**, Florence was, two centuries later, the chosen city of the Renaissance masters, **Leonardo da Vinci, Michelangelo, Sandro Botticelli, Raphael,** and **Donatello**. Indeed, Florence's name is almost synonymous with the Renaissance's flowering. Florence is now a living museum, housing 57 museums and palaces, including the exquisite **Uffizzi** and the **Palazzo Pitti**. Many of **Michelangelo's** buildings grace Florence's streets, including the **Laurentian Library** (started in 1524), which houses **Leonardo da Vinci's notebooks** and a fifth century **Virgil** manuscript.

Florence, meaning The Flourishing Town, was built by the Romans in the first century BC, laid out in rectangular blocks and graced by a central forum and temple. Amidst the warring of the ruling **Guelfs** and **Ghibellines** of the thirteenth and fourteenth centuries, Florence was thriving, minting its first **florin** in the thirteenth century, and eventually making its bankers Europe's most powerful. Great minds like **Dante Alighieri, Petrarch** and **Giovanni Boccaccio** popularized the Tuscan dialect.

In 1610, the great astronomer **Galileo Galilei** discovered the four largest moons of Jupiter while observing the heavens from a Florentine tower. Having confirmed **Copernicus'** idea that the Earth revolves around the Sun, Galileo was admonished by the church and finally confined to his villa outside the city until his death in 1642.

The great **Medici family** of powerful and prestigious bankers took over in 1421, using family wealth and diplomacy as tools for the building of Renaissance Florence. Florence and Tuscany were united under three centuries of Medici rule, characterized by artistic taste and fashion. The **Palazzo Vecchio**, the palace of the Medici family, is still Florence's centerpiece. In 1533, Catherine de' Medici — later the inventor of French cuisine — married **Henri of Valois**, who would rise to rule France as **Henri II**, with Catherine as queen.

Florence retains the historical pattern of the original city, stretching 40 square miles (105 square kilometers) over the **Arno River's** valley. Home to 453,000 residents, Florence is surrounded by the hills of **Tuscany** with their wealth of vineyards, farms and orchards.

The center of the ancient Roman city is now the **Piazza della Republica**, which retains its position between the religious center of Florence and the civic center. It was formerly the **Old Market of Medieval times**, which was destroyed in 1880 for a more contemporary design that is bordered by elegant cafés, booksellers and boutiques.

An exquisite view of Il Duomo and the Palazzo Vecchio.

Geneva, in its spectacular setting on Lac Leman, is the location for many of the most important international conferences. It is also the headquarters for more agencies of the **United Nations** than any other city outside New York, although **Switzerland** never joined the UN. It has had a history of intellectual and commercial links with the world's most powerful nations.

In the sixteenth century, the city of Geneva became the center of the Calvinist movement, and this age of strict morality has defined Geneva's character ever since, making its international relations invaluable. The city has grown into a highly cosmopolitan center of commerce and services, with its population of 378,000 defined as one third native, one third Swiss from other cantons and one third foreign, including French, German and Italian immigrants.

Geneva began as an old world European city on an easily defendable hill located where the outlet of **Lake Geneva** connects to the **Rhone River**, which bisects the city. The symbolic heart of Geneva is still the hill, which the **Cathedral of St. Peter** dominates. Its narrow streets are lined with medieval houses and contemporary government buildings. At the foot of the hill, Geneva has reclaimed land from the Rhone and the lake and built a shopping district that gives way to nineteenth century suburbs and working-class homes.

The city was fortified by **Allobrogian Celts** as early as 58 BC. It served as the first capital for the **German Burgundian Kingdom** from 443 to 534. With the extinction of the line of **Genevese counts** in 1401, Geneva was transferred to the **Counts of Savoy**. After the last ruling bishop fled the city in 1533, Geneva declared herself a state. To keep the bishop at bay and avoid the domination of Savoy and Bern, Geneva declared herself Protestant, alienating herself from the Roman Catholic Swiss cantons.

It was this choice that opened Geneva to **John Calvin**, the French theologian who arrived in Geneva as it was evolving into a modern city-state. His strict form of Protestantism, sometimes brutal enough to support the execution of nonbelievers, grew legendary. Scholars from all over Europe attended his seminars and academies, spreading the Calvinist movement.

France annexed the city in 1798, and it came under **Napoleon's** protection. The aristocratic republic was back in power by 1814, but in 1846, the working class revolted, overthrowing the regime. The radical party, led by **James Fazy**, drew up the new Constitution of 1848.

Later, still during the nineteenth century, the city was reformed with railway lines and the establishment of the **Bank of Geneva**. The **International Red Cross** was founded in Geneva in 1864, and the **League of Nations** established its headquarters here in 1919. Since **World War II**, Geneva has emerged as a major conference center.

Geneva and the Jet d'Eau as viewed from across the lake.

33. GLASGOW, SCOTLAND
Founded in 1180

Glasgow, Scotland evolved from a religious community, which was settled by **St. Kentigern** in 550, into a trading center for Highland and Lowland Scotland. By the eighteenth century, an important international trading port had developed on Glasgow's narrow **Clyde River**. The port first did business in American tobacco, but when the American Revolution destroyed the tobacco market in the 1770s, the manufacturing of cotton goods became the dominant industry. The Cotton Famine in America, caused by the **American Civil War** (1861-1865), cut off the entire supply of raw cotton, taking down the city's four largest textile firms.

Glasgow's main industries shifted again, to shipbuilding, which made the city world famous, to chemical manufacturing, which dominated the city's commerce during the **Industrial Revolution**, and to coal mining. A cheap form of iron was discovered under parts of the city in the 1840s, and Glasgow easily supported itself on its manufacture, feeding Britain's booming railroad industry. At the end of **World War I**, Glasgow's industry was again shaken by the decreased demand for iron, so the city expanded its industrial base. Glasgow now covers an area of 76 square miles (197 square kilometers) along the Clyde's banks. The river has been dredged and deepened, enabling ships to glide into the city's center, and the banks are now crowded with shipyards.

Glasgow is the largest city in Scotland, with wide streets, open squares and great buildings of Scottish stone. The oldest home in the city, the **Provand's Lordship**, was built in 1471, and **St. Mungo's Cathedral** (1221) stands on the spot of the original first century chapel. **Glasgow University** was founded in 1451, and the main museum, **the Hunterian**, was established in 1807.

St. Rollox works, Glasgow, circa 1800. This was then the largest chemical factory in Europe.

As Mark Greenberg wrote in the introduction to his study of the city, "Like thirteenth century Venice, **The Hague** owed its vast wealth to the sea; and like fifteenth century Florence, it used that wealth to attract the greatest convocation of artistic talent assembled anywhere since the High Renaissance..."

Originally the site of a hunting lodge used by the **Counts of Holland**, The Hague became **Count William II's** home when he built a brick castle called the **Old Hall** in 1248. Later, William's son, **Foris V**, built the massive **Ridderzaal**, or Hall of the Knights. It stands today with the other buildings of the **Binnenhof**, the interior court, at the city's heart. A commercial district developed around the court in the thirteenth and fourteenth centuries, and in 1350, the man-made **Hofvijver Lake** was dug on the north side.

The Hague became the royal residence for the **House of Orange** in 1585, along with the States-General and the government of the province of Holland. The Hague was then fortified by a system of canals in 1616, which continued to border the city all the way into the mid-nineteenth century.

The Hague amassed immense power and wealth through its port's trade, flooding the House of Orange with "curios and treasures from around the world," and drawing artists who would shape painting styles through today. The Hague became the seat of government of the **Kingdom of the Netherlands** after the end of Napoleonic rule, and the **Hague Peace Conferences of 1899** and **1907** made the city a permanent center of international law. The **Peace Palace** was completed in 1913 with an endowment from Andrew Carnegie.

The Hague is perhaps best known internationally as the home of the **International Court of Justice**. Originally established by the **League of Nations** after **World War I**, the Court became an agency of the **United Nations** after **World War II**.

The **Mauritshuis Royal Art Gallery** holds the works of **Rembrandt, Vermeer, Jan Steen** and others, and the **Haags Commune Museum** holds the world's largest collection of **Piet Mondrian's** paintings. In their company is the **Protestant New Church** (1654). The twentieth century has seen an increase of light industry, including a new focus on banking, trade and insurance in this city of 678,000 citizens.

The historic Peace Palace at The Hague, circa 1940.

41

One of the busiest ports in **Germany**, **Hamburg** is Germany's second most populous city after Berlin. With an area of 292 square miles (755 square kilometers) on the **Elbe River**, the city has a vast cultural character, supported by the reputations of artists like **Mendelssohn** and **Brahms** and director and performer **Gustaf Grundgens** of the **Deutsche Schauspielhaus**. A powerful publishing industry has flourished here since the seventeenth century. The city's physical character is enhanced by a system of canals that weave through it. Hamburg also features numerous lakes, parks, and excellent museums, including the **Kunsthalle** (1868), the **Museum of Arts and Crafts** (1877) and the **Museum of Ethnology and Prehistory** (1878).

Hamburg's beginnings are fairly tragic and romantic in themselves. Between the Elbe River and the Alster, the **Hammaburg Castle** was built in 825 and became the residence of **Archbishop Ansgar,** who made Hamburg the base of his Christian influence over northern Europe's pagan residents. Though the young city was burned to the ground by **Norse Vikings** in 845, it was steadily rebuilt, only to be burnt eight more times within the next 300 years.

By the thirteenth century, **the Hanseatic League**, including the Baltic trading towns of **Lubeck, Breslau** and **Danzig,** had strengthened the economic health of the united north German cities. Trade was booming, and Hamburg became a major port for trade between Russia and Flanders by controlling and safeguarding the Elbe River. Though the Hanseatic League was dissolved at the end of the Middle Ages, Hamburg continued to grow, surpassing Lubeck and founding the Hamburg stock exchange in 1558. Between 1616 and 1625, Hamburg built up her own defenses while supporting public institutions, like the orphanage built in 1604 and the hospital founded for the poor in 1605.

By 1625, the city was successfully fortified and could continue to trade through the worst of the **Thirty Years' War** (1618-1648), which left other cities impoverished. Only when **Napoleon** attacked in 1810 did Hamburg lose her advantage. She was annexed to the French Empire, but after Napoleon's fall was she able to regain her prosperity as "a Free and Hanseatic City." Trade then expanded into Africa, the Americas and Asia.

Since rebuilding the damage sustained during **World War II** to its port, Hamburg has regained its position as Germany's major port and one of northern Europe's most important ports. The five principal churches have been built and rebuilt after the fires, many elegant suburbs have sprung up along the banks of **Aussenalster Lake**, and a collection of fine, patrician houses are used by Hamburg's many consulates.

A pre World War II aerial view of the port of Hamburg.

Hanoi, now the capital of **Vietnam**, was the capital of the **Democratic Republic of Vietnam** (North Vietnam) from 1954 to 1976. Settled since prehistoric times on the **Red River's** western bank, the city had many buildings that equaled or surpassed those that remain: the **Co Loa Citadel**, dating from the third century BC, the **Temple of Literature**, dedicated to **Confucius** in 1070, the **Mot Cot Pagoda**, built in 1049, the **Temple of the Trung Sisters**, built in 1142, and the works of Hanoi's museums, which include the **National Museum, the Revolutionary Museum** and the **Army Museum**.

Hanoi is accustomed to the political spotlight. Chinese conquerors often chose the city (then called **Dong Kinh** and changed by Europeans to **Tonquin**) as their center, and during the reign of the **Ly Dynasty** (1009-1225), Hanoi was made the capital of Vietnam, which it remained until the **Nguyen**, the final Vietnamese dynasty, moved the capital to **Hue** in 1802. The French also favored Hanoi, making it the capital of **Indochina** in 1902 because of its location near southern China. Administration continued from Hanoi during the Japanese occupation, which lasted from 1940 to 1945. At the end of **World War II**, the Japanese left, and **Ho Chi Minh** and his **Viet Minh** guerrillas seized the city. The French returned to reassert their colonial power, but faced long years of Viet Minh insurgency, which led to their withdrawal in 1954. After the French left, Vietnam was divided into the **Republic of Vietnam** (South Vietnam), with its capital in **Saigon**, and Ho Chi Minh's Democratic Republic of Vietnam, with Hanoi as its capital.

North Vietnam sponsored the **National Liberation Front (Viet Cong)**, who waged a long-term guerrilla war in South Vietnam with an eye toward reunification, finally achieving this in 1975. From 1964 to 1973, the United States intervened in opposition to the Viet Cong with massive firepower. During the **Vietnam War**, Hanoi was attacked sporadically by American aircraft, but escaped the kind of devastation that was wrought on Viet Cong-held areas in South Vietnam. After the American withdrawal, North Vietnam used conventional rather than guerrilla operations to force the absorption of South Vietnam into the Democratic Republic of Vietnam.

After the end of the American trade embargo in the early 1990s, Hanoi, an industrial and agricultural city with over three million citizens, stood to become an important economic center in Southeast Asia.

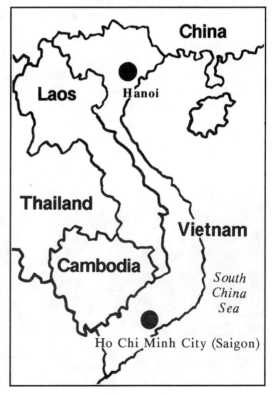

43

Havana, Cuba's capital and choicest port, was once the rendezvous point for Spanish ships that were full of treasure and bound for Europe from the New World. The city was also the starting point for Spanish conquistadors, who embarked from here in the sixteenth century to exploit the Americas' riches from Florida to Peru.

Havana was founded on Cuba's marshy southern coast in 1515. In 1519, the site was abandoned to the mosquitos and swamp animals, and Havana relocated to its present position on the north coast, where it now covers 286 square miles (740 square kilometers). With land on either side, defense was possible, even from sixteenth century English, French and Dutch sea marauders. In 1592, the governor's residence was transferred to Havana from **Santiago**, and Havana became the de facto capital. But in the eighteenth century, the end of the British siege under Admiral Sir George Pocock left Havana in British hands as a spoil of war for six months, until the treaty ending the **Seven Years' War** restored Havana to the Spanish. The city grew into a major trading port, and in 1898, Cuba was one of the last nations to declare its independence from Spain, although American intervention was required to evict the Spanish.

By the middle of the twentieth century, Havana, with its beautiful beaches and sophisticated nightlife, had become one of the world's most popular resort cities. With this came corruption; the city's notorious gambling casinos became controlled by American organized crime interests, who influenced the unscrupulous Cuban government. In 1959, **Fidel Castro** led a popular uprising which seized President **Fulgencio Batista**'s government. Castro closed the casinos, bringing down the curtain on Havana's celebrated nightclub scene. Under Castro's heavily socialized economic system, most businesses are controlled by the state, but education is compulsory and free. Castro's economic experiment, which survived for many years because of Soviet financial support, began to unravel after the Soviet Union's collapse, so Cuba began accepting American dollars as hard currency in the early 1990s. This in turn led to a partial rejuvenation of Havana's long-dormant role as a tourist mecca. **Carnival** is still celebrated by Havana's 2.1 million citizens, while the Tropicana nightclub still features wildly dressed dancers performing to pop songs, which, while often anti-American, are mostly imported from that country.

Today, the older part of Havana, originally protected by forts and walls, is still a city of narrow streets, cobblestone plazas and ornate iron balconies. Its architectural style combines the beauty of grand, baroque churches and Spanish colonial buildings with contemporary commercial structures. West of Old Havana, President Castro's major speeches are delivered from the **Plaza de la Revolucion**.

Looking down El Prado in Havana, circa 1930.

Helsinki is not only **Finland's** leading seaport, it is also its capital. While today's Helsinki is the picture of healthy stability, the city has not been immune from danger during the volatile twentieth century. In the 1940 **"Winter War,"** Soviet Armies invaded Finland, threatening Helsinki and costing Finland **Western Keralia** and the **Petsamo Region**. During the Cold War's dark years, Helsinki lived under the Soviet Union's shadow, looming just a few hours away.

Helsinki was founded twice, once at the mouth of the Vantaa River by **King Gustav Vasa of Sweden**, and again in 1640, when it was moved three miles south to the Gulf of Finland's edge, allowing open access to the sea. Bordering small, natural harbors and sitting on the far southern peninsula, Helsinki is the most northerly of continental European capitals.

Burned to the ground in 1713 after three years of plague that decimated its population, and again in 1808, after Russian troops invaded, Helsinki was slow to rise to its current prominence. In 1812, the Russian tsar **Alexander I** named Helsinki the capital of the Russian **Grand Duchy of Finland**. By 1919, when Finland declared its independence from Russia, Helsinki had grown immensely, both in population, which had reached 100,000 in 1890, and in importance. The great neoclassical architect **C.L. Engel** had reconstructed the central city, building the **state council building**, the central building of **Helsinki University** and the **Lutheran Cathedral** around Senate Square. Very little remains of Russian style architecture in the city.

Helsinki's excellent harbors and good railway lines increased trade, enabling the **Wartsila shipyard** and the **Arabian porcelain factory**, one of Europe's largest, to develop international reputations. Finland's first president was elected by the Helsinki parliament in 1919, ending the bloody civil war that brought Finland's independence.

"The white city of the north," as Helsinki is called for its pale granite buildings, drew 69 nations to the 1952 **Olympic Games** held in the **Helsinki Stadium**. Annually, the city hosts a festival of world-famous orchestras and artists. Year-round the city's half-million citizens enjoy guests at the city theater, which was designed by **Timo Penttila**, and at the concert building, which was designed by **Alvar Aalto**.

Helsinki has hosted many important international conferences, including one in 1975 that led to the **Helsinki Accords**, which were an attempt to lessen tensions and establish human rights standards between the Soviet Union and Western blocs.

The shopping district, Aleksi Street, in Helsinki.

Hiroshima's position as an historically important symbol is its key to prominence among the world's family of great cities. Hiroshima was the first of two Japanese cities to withstand the only **atomic bombs** ever dropped in warfare. "**Little Boy**" was dropped on the small city of Hiroshima on August 6, 1945. Along with the "**Fat Man**," which was dropped on **Nagasaki** three days later, the atomic bomb caused **Japan's** surrender, subsequently ending **World War II**.

The city now shows few signs of the attack. Only the shattered dome and shell of the former **Hall of Industrial Promotion** still stands, reminding the populace of the city's near destruction at the U.S. Army's hands. Throughout the city, new construction and a growing industrialization have covered the scars, and the city's 1.1 million citizens are served by administrative offices, public utility centers and a university.

The capital of **Hiroshima prefecture** in southwestern **Honshu**, Hiroshima is situated on the delta of the **Ota River**, where it was founded as a castle town in the sixteenth century. The city grew into a **military center** in 1868, and retained that status until 1945's atomic bomb attack. After the blast, Hiroshima suffered raging fires that were fanned by the rugged winds that followed. Subsequent radiation poisoning contributed to a death toll that exceeded 40,000.

After the city was rebuilt, Hiroshima became a center for a movement dedicated to a nuclear weapons ban. The **Atomic Bomb Casualty Commission** (1947) studies radiation's biological and medical effects. In 1957, the **Hiroshima Castle** was rebuilt and established as a museum of city history. Hiroshima has covered over its empty, burnt plains with functional, squarish buildings and pristine new streets. It has survived and thrived in recent years and continues to grow as a sound economic and industrial power within Japan.

An aerial view of the harbor at Hiroshima.

Hong Kong is a Chinese port city, leased to Britain as a Crown colony under a 99-year-lease, expiring in 1997. Under British rule, the city evolved into one of Asia's most important financial centers. Thanks to **Victoria Harbour's** wonderful natural port, Hong Kong is one of the world's most important commercial hubs. It covers 412 square miles (1,071 square kilometers) of land that is stretched mainly over Hong Kong Island (and **234** other, smaller islands), the southern area of the **Kowloon Peninsula**, and the southern coast of mainland China, east of the **Pearl River Estuary**. Ancient pottery fragments, rings and bronze pieces are evidence of Hong Kong's early settlement. The **Cantonese** probably arrived in about 100 BC, followed by the **Hakka** and the **Hoklo**, who settled in the mid-seventeenth century, when the final conflicts between the ancient **Ming Dynasty** and the young **Ch'ing Dynasty** were being fought here. In 1821, the British established a post at the small fishing village on **Hong Kong Island**. Its excellent harbor became a safe haven for opium-carrying ships sailing the **Far East trade routes**. To break the opium influence, **China** waged the **First Opium War** (1839-1842), losing Hong Kong Island to Britain in the **Treaty of Nanking**. China also lost the **Second Opium War** (1856-1860), and in the **Convention of 1898** signed the agreement leasing 235 islands plus the New Territories to Britain for 99 years.

Under British influence, Hong Kong Island became China's administrative and economic heart. However, in its **Kowloon hills**, small, compact villages can still be found, often walled, complete with the **feng-shui woods**, "sacred groves," which are inhabited by native forest trees. The once ubiquitous rice paddies have been nearly wiped out by farmers switching to fish farming and cultivating vegetables.

The governor, appointed by the United Kingdom, manages Hong Kong, whose trade has expanded rapidly, especially its tailoring industry, which has become world renowned. Textiles and clothing are the primary exports to the United States, which is Hong Kong's main market. Alongside its economic success, the population has expanded, from 5,000 in 1842 to 5.8 million in 1990.

Under British rule, the Chinese of Hong Kong celebrate both Western holidays and traditional Eastern festivals. The **Dragon Boat Festival, the Mid-Autumn Festival** and the **Chinese New Year** are joined by the Western Christmas and New Year. The **Hong Kong Arts Festival** is an annual celebration of culture, and performers like the **Hong Kong Philharmonic Orchestra**, the **Hong Kong Chinese Orchestra** and the **City Contemporary Dance Company** are among China's best. Hong Kong also supports a thriving film industry, showcased at the **Hong Kong International Film Festival** (1977).

A Hong Kong street scene, circa 1930.

The **Texas Writers Program** wrote of Texas' largest city, "the story of **Houston** has always been that of its port....Today, giant, oceangoing vessels, hailing one another with deep-throated whistles, slide along its inland tidal waterway...."

By the early 1980s, Houston's port, the US's third largest in tonnage moved, was annually handling more than 80 million tons of foreign, coastal and canal shipping. Aside from its trade, its crops of rice, cotton and cattle, as well as its immense resources of natural gas, sulfur, lime and salt, Houston is one of the nation's leading oil centers. Discovered in the area in 1901, oil has made many Texans rich and given the city a firm economic base. Houston, located on the southeastern edge of **Texas**, is linked to the **Gulf of Mexico** by the **Houston Ship Channel**. The inland port city combines the vine covered oak trees, great cottonwoods and elms of the lush South with magnolias and bluebonnets, reminding visitors of Houston's surrounding rich prairies and mossy bayou shores. This city features some of Texas' greatest universities, from **Rice University** (1912) to the **University of Houston** (1927) and **The Texas Medical Center** (1945). The city also supports its own professional **symphony orchestra**, as well as the **Grand Opera Association**, the **National Space Hall of Fame** and the **Astrodome**, home to its football team, the **Oilers**.

The relatively young city was founded by **Sam Houston** on the destroyed site of **Harrisburg** in 1836, after his Texas Army freed the state by capturing the Mexican General **Santa Ana**. Growth was nearly immediate because young **Augustus C.** and **John K. Allen** convinced the **Republic of Texas'** first Congress to make Houston the state capital. The decision held for two years before the state government left Houston, which grew slowly despite yellow fever epidemics and the **Civil War**, in which Texas was a **Confederate State**. Houston stayed unharmed in the war, although in 1863, the city was briefly threatened by the Union capture of nearby Galveston Island.

Houston continued to flourish after the war, due to its significant rail center, its excellent port, and the national importance of Texas oil. Houston's 1.6 million residents have been described as wildcat investors, risky and dynamic, as well as cordial family people who grace their homes with excellent gardens. Houston today is a city of modern architectural wonders like massive skyscrapers and lavish hotels. Houston is also home to **NASA's Johnson Space Center**, where all astronauts receive training and all manned space flights are planned and controlled.

The control room at NASA's
Lyndon B. Johnson Space Center in Houston.

As **Byzantium**, **Istanbul** was called "the New Rome" in 330 AD by **Constantine the Great**, who chose it as the capital for the Eastern Roman, or Byzantine, Empire. He did not, however, actually rename it for Rome, but for himself, and the city was known as **Constantinople** for a millennium.

Byzantium was a Greek trading city built on the site of a prehistoric village built by Byzan in 667 BC. It covered about nine square miles (23 square kilometers) of a narrow southern peninsula at the confluence of three important waterways. Along the shores of the **Marmara Sea**, fifth century walls still stand. The **Golden Horn**, the name for the busy waterway between the southern and northern shores, separated the old city, with its requisite seven hills, from the new city, Beyodglu, to the north. The Golden Horn flows into the **Bosporous Sea,** which hugs the southern tip of Asia.

Byzantium was a highly coveted city, captured by **Persian, Ionian** and then **Spartan** forces in 405 BC. **Alexander the Great** enforced **Macedonian** rule in the third century BC, but the Roman Emperor **Septimus Severus** massacred the populace and razed Byzantium in 196 AD, eventually rebuilding it on a grander scale. Under Roman rule, Byzantium remained untouched until Constantine I became head of the entire Roman Empire and chose the grand city as his capital.

Constantinople was to reign as the chief city of the Western world, organized by the Romans, socialized by the Greeks and adorned with the statues plundered from rival cities. The **Hippodrome** was completed, featuring ivory doors and mosaic floors inlaid with precious metals. Religiously, the city's populace was aligned with Constantine, the first Roman emperor to convert to Christianity, although he accepted the practice of pagan and Jewish customs within his city.

In 1453, the city fell to the **Ottoman Turks**, who returned it to a position of prestige as the capital of the **Ottoman Empire**. In the nineteenth century, the first bridge was built across the Golden Horn, and the European railroad was extended to the new city of Istanbul in the north. In October 1923, after the defeat of the Ottoman Empire in **World War I** and the establishment of a European-style republic, **Ankara** was chosen as the capital of **Turkey**. Istanbul's 6.6 million residents are now citizens of the **Turkish Republic**, but not residents of the Turkish capital.

Currently Turkey's largest city and seaport, Istanbul's municipal boundaries stretch over 98 square miles (246 square kilometers), covering the banks of the three seas that separate the continents of Europe and Asia. With 25 remaining Byzantine churches, perfectly preserved Corinthian columns, a limestone aqueduct from 366 AD and institutions like the German and French archaeological institutes, contemporary Istanbul is a cultural and historical treasure chest.

The Mosque of Ayiah Sofia in Istanbul.

Jakarta, on the island of Java, is the **Republic of Indonesia's** capital and largest city, focusing its resources on education and a growing financial and industrial economy.

While it was founded as **Batavia** by the Dutch in 1527 and made the capital of the **Netherlands East Indies** in 1619, there is evidence of earlier habitation dating back to the fifth century AD. With its large squares and colonial homes, Jakarta has the look of a European city. It also has an Oriental flavor, or "Indische" style, evidenced in its generous garden lots and wide, tree-lined streets.

In Jakarta's youth, when it was still the city of **Batavia**, it resembled a familiar Dutch town with great city walls and canals. Now, the old city, called **The Kota**, is the main area where these traditional Dutch neighborhoods can still be found. It is the financial heart of the city which is home to a significant part of Jakarta's Chinese population. Here can be found the **Portuguese Church** (1695) and the **old city hall** (1710). In other parts of the city, the houses are commonly built of wood or bamboo mats and called **kampong**, or village houses.

As a center for trade and education, Jakarta has become a modern metropolis of 8.2 million people, covering an area of 228 square miles (590 square kilometers) at the mouth of the **Ciliwung** (Liwung) **River**, where it sits on a low, easily flooded alluvial plain with great swampy areas and a shrinking population of upland forest vegetation.

Jakarta's unique mix of Western and Eastern styles developed over its history of foreign rule, which began with its settlement by the Dutch East India Company in the sixteenth century. There was a period of brief British control during the **Napoleonic Wars**, an occupation by Japanese forces in **World War II**, and a subsequent occupation by Allied troops. Indonesia declared her independence at the war's end in 1945, but the Netherlands insisted on continued control, so independence was not actually achieved until 1949.

Batavia, renamed Jakarta, then experienced a great building boom. In 1950, the **Universitas Indonesia** was founded, and the **Hotel Indonesia** and **Sanayan Sports Complex** were built for the **Asian Games** of 1962. Along with sports, Jakarta celebrates traditional arts like **wayang dance** and drama, **gamelan music** and **wayang puppet shows**. In the annual **Jakarta Fair**, performances celebrating all the cultures of Indonesia are showcased.

A canal in Jakarta, circa 1920, when the city was known as Batavia.

From its founding by the early **Canaanites, Jerusalem** has been honored as a sacred city by the followers of three major religions: **Judaism, Christianity** and **Islam**. Jerusalem has been **Israel's** capital and a Jewish holy land since its capture in 1000 BC by **King David**, who united the twelve tribes of Israel and became King of the Jews. During Rome's 386-year occupation, **Jesus Christ** (4 BC-28 AD) was crucified in Jerusalem, making it the Christian holy land as well. Because Jerusalem surrendered to **Omar** and the **Moslem Arabs**

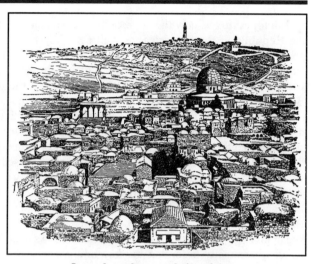

Jerusalem, the sacred city of three world religions: Christianity, Judaism and Islam.

after they laid siege to it in 638, the two mosques and the **Noble Shrine** have become Islam's most sacred sanctuaries.

Jerusalem, with its subtropical weather, encompasses 41 square miles (107 square kilometers) in Israel's center. To the east, it looks down onto the **Dead Sea**, across the **Jordan River** and onto the dry mountains of **Moab**. To the west, it faces the coastal plain heading into the Mediterranean Sea.

The old city, once surrounded by walls built by the **Ottomans** between 1538 and 1540, still exists, though the walls have given way to a ring of major avenues. This core city, which is surrounded by the Jewish, Christian, Muslim and Armenian quarters that comprise the new city, is dominated by a raised platform on which sits the **Herodian Temple Compound**, the site of the first and second Hebrew temples.

For a brief period (1099-1144) during the **Crusades**, the city was under Christian rule. Otherwise, Jerusalem was under Islamic control for 1,280 years, with the Arabs ruling the city from 637 AD to 1517, and the **Ottoman Empire** reigning it until

1917. Placed under British control by a **League of Nations** — and later a **United Nations** — mandate, western Jerusalem became part of the modern state of **Israel**, which was created by the United Nations in 1948. Straddling the border of Israel and **Jordan**, Jerusalem remained split until the **Arab-Israeli War of 1967**, when Israel annexed the Jordanian section and declared the united city as Israel's capital. Today, many of Jerusalem's half-million residents support themselves in government and public service jobs or as skilled laborers in the diamond-cutting, printing and publishing industries. The city's diverse population manages to live peacefully inside the city, although there is a high level of tension between the Israeli population and the **Palestinian people**, upon whose land Israel was superimposed, and who also claim Jerusalem as their capital. A historic peace accord, signed in 1994, has paved the way toward peace by allowing limited Palestinian rule outside of Jerusalem. The future political status of Jerusalem has not, however, been addressed.

Johannesburg is now the largest city in the **Republic of South Africa**, as well as one of the African continent's biggest. It is a city with a past, backed up by a history of friction between the pioneering Dutch **Boers** (farmers), who settled in the surrounding **Transvaal** region, and the British miners, who helped build the city immediately after gold was discovered in 1886 in the nearby **Witwatersrand**. The site that would later become Johannesburg's heart was one of many land plots declared as public diggings. Under commissioners **Johann Rissik** and **Christian Johannes Joubert**, it began to grow into the mining region's major city, eventually becoming the key rail hub for all of Southern Africa.

In 1899, the **Boer War** broke out between the **British Empire** and the **Zuid-Afrikaansche Republiek** (comprised of the Afrikaner Republics of Transvaal and the Orange Free State). The world's sympathies were for the Afrikaners engaged in a valiant war for independence, but by 1900 they had lost, and the mines were turned over to the British.

In 1922, white miners went on strike to protest the use of black Africans in semi-skilled labor positions. The strike cost more than 200 lives before it was suppressed, but it also began a period of tension that led to the apartheid laws of the 1940s. These were not reversed until 1994, when black majority rule was instituted in the Republic of South Africa.

Johannesburg had a growth spurt that increased its boundaries to 104 square miles (269 square kilometers) by the 1970s. As Johannesburg grew, racial segregation created a white South African metropolis. Blacks were officially restricted to areas like **Soweto,** a neighboring black township governed by the Johannesburg, but not actually a part of the municipality. In 1956, 100,000 non-whites were commanded to leave their city homes within a year to make room for more white citizens.

In 1994, South Africa voted **Nelson Mandella** into office as its first black president. Though race relations are still being solidified, Johannesburg now enjoys the cultural wealth of a free cosmopolitan population. Along with Johannesburg's 60 percent black population, Europeans, Asians and Jews comprise its 1.6 million populace.

Gold mining, which first generated Johannesburg, is now conducted elsewhere, but the city has remained South Africa's business capital.

The Johannesburg skyline.

Kiev is called "the mother of Russian cities" for its position at the center of the first eastern Slavic state, the **Kievan Rus**, which was founded by the Scandinavian **Varangians**, believed to be the original settlers of the Ukrainian and Russian states. Due to its wealthy port frequented by sailors travelling ancient trade routes, Kiev has long been respected for its "noble past as the enlightened capital of medieval Russia."

Kiev's history begins with three mythological brothers, **Kiy, Shchek** and **Khoriv**, who each built a settlement on one of three hills. These hills, divided by a stream named for their sister **Lybed**, constituted the city of Kiev.

In 988, Christianity took hold in Kiev, as evidenced by chronicles stating that the city had more than 400 churches. Famed for its art and the frescoes and mosaics adorning its churches, Kiev was much desired by **Batu**, the grandson of Genghis Khan, who, along with his **Mongol warriors**, invaded and destroyed much of Kiev in 1240. **Lithuania**, who captured Kiev in 1362, gave the lands and city to Poland in 1569, under the Union of Lublin between the two countries. In 1793, under **Catherine the Great**, the city was brought into the **Russian Empire**. Kiev subsequently survived the social unrest that brought the strikes of 1905 and the **Russian Revolution of 1917**. The Germans captured the city on September 1941, massacring more than 30,000 Jews, POWs and partisans in a nearby ravine known as **Baby Yar**. Liberated in 1943, Kiev was honored with the Order of Lenin and the title of Hero City. After **World War II**, Kiev grew into a modern industrial city, now covering 62 square miles (156 square kilometers) and supporting a population of over 2.6 million people.

With the Soviet Empire's dissolution, an independent **Ukraine** was established in 1991 with Kiev as its capital, enabling the city to step out from under **Moscow's** shadow and return to its position as an important city in world politics.

From the left bank of the **Dnieper River**, among the city's many factories, one can look over to where the ancient **Upper Town** was built along the bluffs of the precipitous right bank. Golden domes and bell towers can be seen, and although the ancient city's body was rebuilt after **World War II**, remaining historical monuments can still be found there. The **Cathedral of St. Sophia**, with its five domes, contains the tomb of **Yaroslav**. The Baroque **Church of St. Andrew** survives from the mid-eighteenth century, and the ruins of the **Golden Gate** date back to the eleventh century. The city's museums, its covered market, and Kiev's terraced gardens surround the old city. North of it, **Podol**, the former trading center and Jewish quarter, contains the principal buildings of the Ukrainian government, including the glass-domed palace of 1936 that housed the Supreme Soviet of the Ukrainian SSR during the Soviet era.

A 1930s view of the Lavra Monastery in Kiev.

Kyoto, Japan's fourth largest city and capital for over 1,000 years, between 794 and 1868 AD, was founded as **Heian-kyo** ("Capital of Peace and Tranquility") by the emperor **Kammu**. Now having a population of 1.5 million, Kyoto is respected as a Japanese center of culture and traditional crafts. It is the Japanese hub of **Buddhism**, with 1,660 Buddhist temples, and a major heart of shintoism, with more than 400 Shinto shrines. Kyoto's major industry for centuries has been silk weaving, with the Fushimi district producing some of the nation's finest sake (rice wine). The city is known as the birthplace of traditional Japanese drama. Stages still offer performances of original **No plays**, and the nation's **Kabuki season**, much like opera season in the United States, commences with the annual opening performance at the **Minami-za**.

Kyoto is an artistic treasure.

The city lies between the Katsura and Kamo Rivers on the island of **Honshu**. The emperor Kammu designed Heian-kyo within a basin of hills and mountains, based on the Chinese idea that a city must be protected at its northern corners, where evil spirits can gain access.

Among peaceful Kyoto's ancient architectural treasures are the **Kyoto Imperial Palace** and the **Nijo Castle**, both surrounded by exquisite gardens, the beautiful **Golden Pavilion** (which, after being burnt down intentionally by a young student in 1950, was rebuilt exactly as it had been previously), as well as the **Silver Pavilion**, which was built due to the **Ashikaga shoguns'** attraction to **Zen**.

Kyoto was settled by Korean immigrants with silk weaving skills. Under the **Fujiwara family**, who dominated the **Heian period**, the Koreans helped enlarge the city past its natural river borders. The first shogun, **Minamoto Yoritomo**, who took control after the decline of the Fujiwara, established many Buddhist temples in the twelfth century. Zen developed under the samurai (warriors), and the No theatre, tea ceremony and flower arranging arts flourished under the aristocratic class in the fourteenth and fifteenth centuries. The city's exceptional collection of historical arts include the women's writings from the original city of Heian-Kyo, considered some of the liveliest writings of any age.

The **Tokugawa shogunate** moved the political center to **Edo**, (Tokyo) in the seventeenth century. The Imperial Court stayed in control of ceremony in the city until the arrival of **Matthew Perry** and the 1853 collapse of **Tokugawa**. Kyoto again became a political center, until the young Meiji emperor set up his new residence in the new capital of Tokyo. Even without political power, Kyoto remains precious to Japanese citizens, who all try to visit the city at least once.

Lagos, the largest city in sub-Saharan Africa, was the capital of Lagos state in **Nigeria** until 1975, when it was made the federal capital of Nigeria, a position it lost to **Abuja** in December of 1991.

Lagos was not always an important city for Nigeria. Founded in 1472 by the **Portuguese**, who maintained good relations with the Yoruban obas (kings), Lagos grew very slowly until it was granted a slaving monopoly. The British, attempting to break the active trade, outlawed slavery in the nineteenth century, which only succeeded in forcing it underground, where it functioned secretly in Lagos' private port. As a small, rarely visited city, Lagos could hide its slave trade, even after 1851, when a British attack overthrew the current oba. The slave trade continued until 1961, when Lagos came under British control.

The city was a British Crown colony and part of the **British Empire's West African Settlement** from 1876 to 1874, when it became part of the **Gold Coast Colony**. In 1906, it was added to the **Protectorate of Southern Nigeria**, and in 1914, when Southern Nigeria was joined with Northern Nigeria, Lagos was made the capital of the **Colony and Protectorate of Nigeria**.

The one-time capital city remains the educational and cultural magnet for Nigerian citizens. It covers only 56 square miles (145 square kilometers), a system of bridged islands that act as its nation's chief port. Industries include auto assembly and food and beverage production, as well as various types of paint, soap and textile manufacturing. The administrative offices of many government agencies are in Lagos, as are the headquarters of the Federal Radio Corporation of Nigeria and the Nigerian Television Authority.

Lagos' system of islands is comprised mainly of **Lagos, Iddo, Ikoyi** and **Victoria Islands**. All of low-lying Lagos is linked over water by bridges. The original settlement, which was home to **Yoruba fisherman** until the Portuguese landed in 1472, is on the northwestern tip of Lagos Island. Lagos' populace has experienced such a population growth (up to 1.4 million in 1990) and such extreme poverty that its original site, characterized by narrow streets, is now an expanding slum area. The heart of the city, including the main business district, exists on the southwestern shore of Lagos Island. Here, the city's financial, commercial and educational wealth is visible among a growing number of high-rise buildings. The **University of Lagos** (1962), the **National Library** and the **National Museum**, all located in the city or its surrounding suburbs, increase Lagos' importance as a cultural center and add style to its established position as an industrial one.

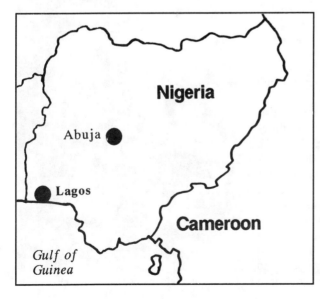

Metropolitan **Lima, Peru's** capital, has affectionately been called "the octopus" for its sprawling size, which measures 120 square miles (310 square kilometers). Lima's 1990 population of 5.8 million equals about one-fourth of Peru's entire populace. As Peru's commercial and industrial center, Lima accounts for three-fifths of the country's industrial output and four-fifths of the nation's consumer purchases.

Backed by the **Andes Mountains** to the west and surrounded by the coastal desert's barren, yellow sands, Lima is an urban oasis that was once the only contact point between the nation and the rest of the faraway world. Founded by conquistador **Francisco Pizarro** in 1535 on Peru's Pacific coast, the Spanish city is surrounded by the religious and cultural sites of **pre-Incan** and **Incan civilizations**. Lima, chosen over the old Incan city of **Cuzco** for its coastal location, its navigable link to Spain, was developed into the capital of the new **Viceroyalty of Peru**, growing slowly into a royal center of wealth and power. Peru was the last country in South America to declare independence, which it did in July, 1821.

The image of contemporary Lima, with its modern overpopulation and poverty, contrasts with the charm of the old city that is partly enclosed by seventeenth century walls. Lima's center is a city of new shopping centers, factories and business offices, while the old city features restored colonial buildings, like the **Archbishop's Palace** and the **Torre Tagle Palace**. Lima's outlying suburbs are shanty towns that once bordered the city until waves of immigration brought one third of today's metropolitan citizenship from rural areas. The towns, built on numerous farms and small abandoned plots, began as clusters of cardboard and wicker shacks that sometimes grew into neighborhoods of small brick houses and gardens.

Lima is divided into the provinces of **Lima** and **Callao**, which are, in turn, divided into forty-five autonomous political districts. Around the two principal squares in Lima (**Plaza de Armas** and **Plaza Bolivar**), the colonial city's enclosed wooden balconies and reproduced **French Empirical** flourishes still exist, while in the former residential area, old, spacious mansions have been subdivided into accommodations for as many as 50 families. In 1984, the **Metropolitan Council for Greater Lima** was founded in hopes of controlling the effects of massive growth.

Lima maintains its status as the cultural center of Peru with the **National University of San Marcos**, the **Pontificia Catholic University** (1917), several daily papers, well-restored burial sites of pre-Inca coastal cultures and the popular sports of football, volleyball, cockfighting and bullfighting.

The Torre-Tagle mansion in Lima, circa 1930.

Lisbon, with its excellent natural harbor, is **Portugal's** largest city as well as its commercial and political capital. Though it is said that the great **Ulysses** founded Lisbon, it is more commonly believed that Lisbon was founded by the **Phoenicians** around 1200 BC. Unfortunately, no proof exists for either theory, leaving Lisbon with both a romantic and a practical history that has influenced everything in Lisbon from the ornamental Gothic architecture, developed in Portugal, to the logical development of modern grided streets and squares. The city's character swings between these two extremes, from the timeless old city's maze of tiny avenues to the modern, northern sectors filled with colorful, high-rise buildings for the city's poor.

Lisbon's character is evidenced in its mythology. From the **Church of St. Vincent-Outside-the-Walls**, where the saint's remains are said to have been delivered by a ship piloted by two ravens, to the **saudade**, or melancholy, that lies over Lisbon's 700,000 people, turning them to the mournful singing of the **fado**, the city sentimentally clings to its mythological history and some of its customs. During the June feasts of the popular saints, Lisbon's citizens, costumed like their pagan ancestors, dance all through the midsummer nights.

Although the city's first residents are unknown, stone inscriptions recount the city's municipal status under **Julius Caesar**. From the Romans, the city passed to **the Alani, the Suebi, the Visigoths, the Muslims of North Africa** and **the Moors**, who lost it to the Portuguese in 1147. **King Dinis I** of Portugal founded the **University of Lisbon** in 1290. The Portuguese age of discovery (1415-1578) established the city as a haven for Dutch, English and French traders, who swarmed to the city that hosted **Vasco da Gama**, the explorer who sailed to India and broke the Venetian trade monopoly.

Philip II of Spain took Portugal in 1578, ruling both countries in 1588, when the **Spanish Armada** sailed against England, a long-term Portuguese ally. In 1640, Lisbon's nobles rose up and overthrew the Spanish, freeing their nation and inspiring **Restoration Square**, which was dedicated to their service.

It was in 1755 that Lisbon suffered its worst blow. On November 1, two shocks from a massive earthquake demolished the city, sending fire through over 9,000 buildings and destroying most of the city's unique Gothic architecture, including the **Palace of the Inquisition**, which was never rebuilt.

Lisbon lies on the far western edge of Europe, spanning 32 square miles (84 square kilometers) on a succession of terraces rising from the banks of the **Tagus River** that is called the city's lover for its tenacious hold on its lower lands, which rise steadily onto the varying peaks of the **Sintra Mountains**. It is crossed by the **25th of April Bridge**, western Europe's longest suspension bridge.

The historic Museum of Archeology and Ethnology in Lisbon.

Founded at the mouth of the Mersey River in 1199, **Liverpool** was the chief English port for Irish trade by 1207. An industrial city whose half-million people have a strong work ethic, Liverpool is the **United Kingdom's** sixth largest city.

King John offered a charter for the building of a new town in 1207, and Liverpool grew slowly until the eighteenth century, when a healthy trade with the Americas and the **West Indies** propelled it into a position of great profit. Liverpool built its first dock in 1715. In 1819, the city received the fist transatlantic crossing of a steamship when the **Savannah** arrived from a Georgia port. Liverpool was one of the most important cities during the **Industrial Revolution** and in 1830, the **Liverpool to Manchester Railway** became the first European rail to link two major cities.

Soon the docks were attracting immigrant workers and expanding down the Mersey. By the twentieth century, Liverpool's docks stretched seven miles. After **World War II**, Liverpool and its port began to decline in capital investments and commerce. Though the city no longer wields great financial power, its cultural centers continue to thrive. The symphony orchestra is well-loved, and the **Merseyside Country Museum and Library** is joined by the **Walker Art Gallery**, the **Picton Library** and the **University of Liverpool** (1881). Liverpool is also one of pop culture's hero cities. All six of the original members of **The Beatles** were born and raised in the city's middle class neighborhoods.

The port of Liverpool in its heyday.

When the **British Empire** was at its apogee during **Queen Victoria's** late nineteenth century reign, **London** was the largest city on Earth, as well as the entire world's financial, cultural and social leader. The **Houses of Parliament**, overlooking the **River Thames** and crowned by the tower containing **Big Ben**, were the world's focal point.

In its youth, London was a vital center for the Romans (the original Roman basilica is now the **Leadenhall Market**) and later the Saxons, who founded **St. Paul's Cathedral** in 604 AD. Following the **Norman conquest** of 1066, **William I the Conqueror** built the imposing **White Tower**, the **Tower of London's** centerpiece, as the seat of his power. After fire swept through London in 1136, buildings of stone and tile appeared in the rebuilding. **Henry VIII** (1509-1566) oversaw the reconstruction of the five royal hospitals, established a dockyard at Deptford, converted the York Palace into **Whitehall** and built **St. James' Palace**. Meanwhile, **Westminster's** noblemen were building their homes on the Strand, but only after the great fire of 1666 was London united to its surrounding townships like Westminster. The beloved **Queen Elizabeth I** (1558-1603) ruled with London's "militia, its money, and its love." **Sir Christopher Wren**, the great architect, is immortalized in the city's great buildings, including the flawless St. Paul's cathedral.

London's importance as a commercial center grew as the British Empire expanded. The wealth from the **British East India Company** (1599), as well as trade with much of the world, nourished London's cultural character. Theater, literature and music bloomed for centuries. **William Shakespeare**, possibly the greatest writer in the history of the English language, built his revolutionary and successful **Globe Theatre** here.

London was also technologically in the lead. By 1812, gas lights illuminated London's streets, omnibuses began running in 1829, rail carriages followed within a decade, and the world's first underground railway, powered by electricity, was completed in 1890. While the nineteenth century **Victorian Age** brought in social reforms that modernized the city and eased the pressures of London's increasing population, growth nevertheless continued unchecked, swelling the population to 4.2 million in 1890. Culturally, London was immortalized by its many brilliant scholars and writers, like **Charles Dickens**, who chronicled London at its zenith during the Industrial Revolution. **Wolfgang Mozart** wrote his first symphony in London at eight years of age.

London also hosted the **Olympic Games** in 1908 and again in 1948.

Today, although the British Empire is defunct, London remains the **United Kingdom's** capital, housing a population of 6.7 million. The royal family reigns from **Buckingham Palace**, which has housed England's monarchs ever since Queen Victoria took up residence in 1837.

The tower containing Big Ben.

59

Los Angeles — "the City of Angels" that is known simply as "LA" — was first a sleepy Spanish mission town that evolved into an agricultural municipality of orange groves and truck farms that finally became today's symbolic capital of **California** mythology, as well as the United States' second most populous city, with a population of 3.5 million. LA has an identity that transcends its own borders, even the borders of Los Angeles County, and applies to much of Southern California. Referred to as a mass of "suburbs in search of a city," it is a sprawling, semitropical metropolis of movie moguls, crowded freeways, pop stars, popular writers, world-class celebrities, impoverished ghettos, aerospace factories, Central American immigrants, surfers and would-be film stars.

The city's massive 464 square mile (747 square kilometer) area lies between the **San Gabriel Mountains** on the east and the **Pacific Ocean** on the west. The county of Los Angeles incorporates more than eighty other cities — including **Pasadena** with its **Rose Bowl**, **Anaheim** with its **Disneyland**, **Long Beach**, and the incredibly wealthy **Beverly Hills** — and is criss-crossed by the ubiquitous miles of freeway that oblige Los Angeles' mythical addiction to the automobile.

Hollywood, LA's most famous suburb — and the only one that is actually part of the city — is the birthplace of the American film industry. However, today's filmmaking actually takes place in other suburbs, such as **Burbank.** Within the Hollywood fantasyland, **Marilyn Monroe, James Dean** and **Humphrey Bogart** immortalized their celluloid selves alongside **Mary Pickford, Bette Davis, Elizabeth Taylor** and **Charlie Chaplin**. From **Laurel and Hardy** to **Paul Newman** and **Demi Moore**, all of Hollywood's myths have been made, and some horribly broken, by the fast paced, raunchy, overworked industry that still attracts young Midwestern beauties and sophisticated investors.

Along with its movies, LA is a land of other fantasies. In the 1930s, it was the mecca for Dust Bowl refugees. Their children taught us to surf and race hot rods, and were rock stars like **Frank Zappa** and **The Doors**. The refugees' grandchildren were the San Fernando Valley's **Valley Girls**, with their sun-bleached curls, the drug culture's movers and shakers, in their raunchy leathers, and the roller-skaters of **Venice** and **Santa Monica**.

LA is also California's largest manufacturing center. The oil refining, electronics and aerospace industries have all built factories on the orange groves that in earlier days generated LA's economic base.

Even as Los Angeles remains a fertile ground for fantasy and entertainment, it also maintains a truly enviable archipelago of museums, featuring the excellent **California State Museum of Science**, the **Museum of Natural History**, the fourth largest of its kind in the United States, and the **Norton Simon Museum**, with its collection spanning 2,000 years.

A nostalgic view of Los Angeles, circa 1890.

The modern city of **Luxor**, situated on the east and west banks of the **Nile River** in Upper **Egypt**, was built on the site of **Thebes**, ancient Egypt's powerful capital. Located between deserts that stretch for miles, the city of Thebes flourished on the regenerative powers of the Nile. The Pharaohs ruled here, creating a civilization unlike any the world has ever seen.

Its outlying western desert lands, the ancient "city of the dead," is where all successors of the god **Amon** were buried with the wealth they would carry to the afterlife. It has yielded a rich archeological collection of ancient Egyptian art and records, some dating back to the third millennium BC. The latest excavation is the tomb of the minor Pharaoh, **Tutankhamen**, which is full of gold jewelry, statues and effects.

Covering an area of about six square miles (15 square kilometers) and having 93,000 residents, Thebes sat mainly on the east bank of the rich river valley. On the original site, the oldest monuments date from the eleventh dynasty (2081-1939 BC), when the provincial town became the capital of united Egypt. Thebes' greatest hour was when the **Hyksos** were driven from the nation and the eighteenth dynasty rebuilt the city with Asian spoils. Gardens and regal palaces were built on the Nile's banks. There the pharaohs competed with one another in the finery and adornment of their temples, which were built both for the god Amon and to hold their own remains. These temples were constantly replenished by groups of slaves, who supplied them with fresh grain and gifts for Amon.

Thebes continued to amass great wealth, much of which was dedicated to worship, until the city began to decline with the reign of later Ramessids in the twelfth century BC. The beginning of the **Iron Age** brought Thebes massive inflation, which was partly remedied by plundering older tombs.

Many of Thebes' rulers left tangible legacies for our study. The eighteenth dynasty **temple of Hatshepsut** depicts her miraculous birth from the union of **Queen Ahmes** and Amon. **Amenhotep III** left two great statues that are known as the **Colossi of Memnon**. Nearly 70 feet high and each carved from a solid block of stone, they are famed for their beauty as well as the northern statue's curious habit of emitting one high note on certain mornings. Until its whistling break was patched, the statue was dubbed "the singing Memnon." The great Pharaoh **Ramses II** commissioned representations of great wars, including his own against the Syrian Hittites, as well as scenes from the harvest god's festival. Decorating the outer pylon of his temple, these images survive to this day. Each year, countless tourists visit Luxor to marvel at these and other relics from the ancient civilization.

The entrance to the palace of Luxor.

Machu Picchu is the name given to the exceptionally well-engineered buildings of the old city of **Vilcampampa**, the principal residence of the final four **Inca** warriors. The Inca people were the ruling class of a massive native American empire that encompassed most of **Peru**, Ecuador, Bolivia, Argentina and northern Chile. Their history was only communicated orally, so what we know of Vilcampampa is confined to accounts from Spanish friars, who attempted to convert the sun-worshippers, and to the stories told to Spanish conquistadors, who conquered Peru in 1533.

The story is also told in the amazing ruins discovered in 1911 by explorer **Hiram Bingham**, the first modern scholar to find the old Vilcampampa, which he renamed Machu Picchu after one of the two mountain peaks that shield the city's view.

The Inca first ruled from the existing city of **Cuzco**, until the Spanish Conquest of Peru. To appease the Indian tribes, the Spanish placed young **Manco** on the throne as an Inca. He ruled as a puppet leader until he staged a failed revolt in 1536. Fleeing the capital city, he took men and great wealth into the Andes mountains, where they founded the impenetrable city of **Vitcos**. From 1536 to 1572, Manco and his three sons after him used Viscos as a military hold, and the city of Vilcampampa, nearly invisible behind it, as their cultural and religious center. Vilcampampa was the most valuable and sacred of cities. Fortified by natural cliffs and peaks, it was seen as the protector of the ancient Inca magic.

Here the Inca held off the Spanish, until one by one, each Inca perished. The city then fell to ruins.

The old Vilcampampa was not discovered until 1911 because it was nearly inaccessible. Sitting in a basin between two peaks, **Machu Picchu and Huayna Pic-** chu, it is surrounded by sheer cliffs that lead 2,000 feet down into the rapids of the Urubamba River.

As a race, the Inca were sun-worshippers who trusted their priests to tie the sun to a stone pillar every year on June 21 or 22 so that it would not free itself and never return. The Inca ruler was regarded as the son of the sun. He was waited upon by the **Chosen Women**, the beauties of the tribe. Trained as expert weavers, they were kept isolated until they were sacrificed or married to either the Emperor or one of his nobles.

What's left of the great city is the masterful stonework of a temple, a citadel, the sites of terraced gardens and the remains of more than 3,000 stone steps that linked the worship sites with the residences. Now a valuable tourist attraction, Machu Picchu exists as one of the only pre-Columbian urban centers found nearly intact.

Machu Picchu shortly after its rediscovery.

Madrid, the capital of **Spain**, was chosen as the country's political and cultural center because of its lack of distinction, rather than its geographic location or mineral wealth. The city is now Spain's largest city and lively center of arts and industry.

Beginning as an Arab town, Madrid was transformed into a small Moorish fortress that defended the important city of **Toledo**. It was then captured by the **Castile's King Alfonso VI** in the eleventh century. It was not until **Philip II** officially made the city the national capital in 1607 that Madrid's palaces, churches and public buildings began to transform the little town into an engaging city. If it weren't for Madrid's previous obscurity and neutral position amongst political factions, Philip II, who took the court to Madrid in 1561, may never have chosen the city for his own.

Madrid has no major river, but flatters the shallow **Manzanares River** with grand bridges that are almost laughable in their inappropriate size. The Manzanares, frequently mocked for being nearly dry, is Madrid's only waterway. Resting high on a plateau of the **Iberian Peninsula**, Madrid grew first around the central castle overlooking the river and later developed east over Calle Mayor and Calle de Segovia.

In 1625, the last walls to encircle the city were built. They were destroyed in 1860, by which time Madrid grew four times its earlier size. Since then, the metropolitan area of the city has expanded to 234 square miles (587 square kilometers), and the population has grown from 472,000 in 1890 to 2.9 million in 1990.

The old center of Madrid still appears cramped because of its maze of narrow streets, but around it has grown a modern center that features the internationally renowned **Prado Museum**, the **University of Madrid** and **the Plaza de Sol**, where crowds have consistently gathered for discussion and even revolt. When the French placed **Joseph Bonaparte** on the throne, Madrid's populace rose up against him in 1808, gaining Madrid the title of "Hero City" after **Ferdinand VII's** return.

The people of Madrid follow some of the oldest Spanish traditions alongside modern business practices. Many of the populace still take the long siesta break at midday and entertain themselves in cafés and theaters until very late at night. The bullfights are still popular, and Madrid's creative spirit stays alive. Its artists continue to produce great works of art which rival the magnificent tapestries of the mayor's residence and the paintings of **Bruegel** and **Titian** that hang in the convent of the **Descalzas Reales**.

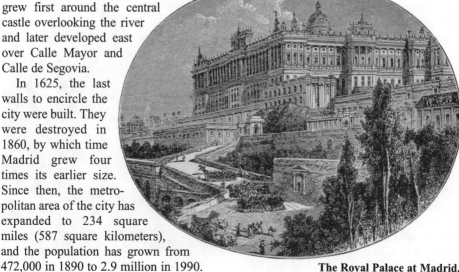

The Royal Palace at Madrid.

Melbourne, the capital of the **Australian** state of **Victoria**, is located on Australia's southern coast, where it is the nation's largest general cargo port. In Australia, Melbourne is second in area only to its rival, **Sydney**, the capital of New South Wales. Melbourne is the only one of Australia's six state capitals to have been established unofficially by enterprise. A fairly young city, Melbourne was founded by pioneer settler **John Batman** in 1835, soon after he signed a treaty with the aboriginal natives. Two months after Batman paid for 500,000 acres at the head of **Port Phillip Bay** with 40 blankets, 30 axes, 100 knives, 50 pairs of scissors, 30 mirrors, 200 handkerchiefs, 100 pounds of flour and six shirts, another pioneer, **John Fawkner**, settled on the Yarra River's banks. There he acquired a large amount of land and established a bookselling business, hotels and a newspaper. Batman died early, ending an active debate over who was the legitimate founder.

Melbourne saw its first immigration wave after gold was discovered nearby in the 1850s. The second wave was stimulated by government programs that supported European immigrants in their attempts to find jobs and learn English. Acting as a haven for people fleeing **World War II**, the city limits strained eastward. Surrounding Melbourne's service-oriented core, a ring of outer suburbs developed. By the end of World War II, the population had reached 100,000. Metal processing, transportation equipment and computer manufacturing greatly boosted the importance of Melbourne's industries, and by 1990, the metropolitan population had grown to 3.1 million.

The city was laid out in a rectangular pattern. Nineteenth century architecture is still evident in the core city, where the **Houses of Parliament** share space with Anglican and Roman Catholic cathedrals. Some of the best ornate ironwork has been preserved; examples of its lacy patterns, which provide shade from the intemperate sun, grace balconies and verandas in the **Carlton District**. After the style fell out of favor in the twentieth century, many visitors began labeling it "gingerbread fussiness."

Melbourne is often viewed, in contrast to Sydney, as more "English," more staid. The Reverend Billy Graham said that Melbourne was the most moral city he had ever visited. Despite this, Melbourne's population includes a healthy ethnic mix of culturally conscious, politically active intellectuals.

With its **National Gallery of Victoria**, its **Victorian Arts Center** and the **Melbourne Concert Hall**, the city is a great supporter of traditional arts. Its extensive parks and grand balconies have preserved an impression of gentility, despite the experimental theater of the 1970s and the proliferation of discos, rock music clubs and a great many pubs.

Collins Street, Melbourne, circa 1920.

Mexico City, named **Tenochtitlan** by its **Aztec** founders in the fourteenth century, is currently the most populated city in the world, with a metropolitan population of 19.5 million living in an area of 571 square miles (1,351 square kilometers). The unchallenged political, economic and cultural center of the **United States of Mexico**, Mexico City has lost its ancient reputation as "the city of palaces" and instead has turned into a metropolis where rush hour can last virtually all day and **Ixtacihuatl** and **Popocatepetl**, the two extinct volcanoes which used to be visible at the foot of the Sierra Nevada, are now consistently obscured by air pollution.

The Aztecs settled in the Mexican valley after they saw the promised sign — an eagle sitting on cactus, eating a serpent — which is today the centerpiece of the Mexican flag. There were about 100,000 inhabitants in 1519, when the Spanish, led by **Hernando Cortés,** arrived to conquer the city. Cortés defeated the Aztec king **Montezuma,** razed the Aztec city in 1521 and constructed a Spanish city over the ruins. To the Spanish, Mexico City became the most important settlement in the Americas, with its jurisdiction reaching north well into today's United States and extending as far south as Panama.

Constant flooding led to the lakes around the central city being filled. By the eighteenth century, elaborate European style facades were being reproduced out of porous volcanic rock in the **baroque style** that characterized the **golden age of architecture**. **Neoclassicism** was subsequently introduced by **Manuel Tolsa**. French dominance took over when **Hapsburg's Archduke Maximilian** came to govern after Napoleon's French troops secured the country from **Benito Juarez**.

The **Mexican Revolution** (1910-1917) left the city in shambles, and when public works resumed, French palaces were replaced with the skyscrapers and other modern buildings that still function today. Mexico City was the site of the **Olympic Games** in 1968. With the oil boom of the late 1970s, the city continued through an age of great expansion until 1985, when an earthquake shook the soft subsoil of the former lakes, killing 7,000 people.

The Aztec chose an island surrounded by lakes as their capital. While the lakes have since been dried out and populated, the original Tenochtitlan continues to dominate as the central area of Mexico City. On its northern side, close to the original Aztec temple, stands the **Metropolitan Cathedral**, and to the east, built over the ruins of the Aztec emperor's palace, stands the **National Palace**.

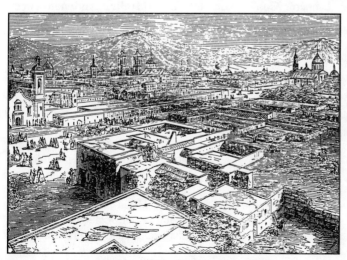

An engraving of Mexico City, circa 1890.

Milan, the second largest city in **Italy** after Rome, is Italy's richest city and also one of Europe's wealthiest. The wealth of this city of 1.4 million people is reflected in its current economic power — spanning such diverse areas as fashion and manufacturing — and its rich heritage, reflected in the marvels of its architecture. From the Gothic **Duomo** (1386), Europe's third-largest cathedral that took five centuries to complete, to the **Palazzo di Brera** (1651), infused with the severe baroque adornments of designer **Francesco Maria Ricchino**, to the fourth century **San Simpliciano**, Milan holds some of Italy's most prized monuments.

Not only does Milan produce great products, it produces great thinkers and artisans. The **Verri Brothers** recommended free trade in the early eighteenth century, **Cesare Beccaria** (1738-94) urged the abolishment of all capital punishment, which the **Grand Duke Leopold of Tuscany** instituted in 1786, and **Alessandro Volta** (1745-1827) invented the electric battery before the turn of the century.

Under **Augustus,** Milan became the second city of the Roman Empire. It was the Vicar of Italy's seat under Emperor **Constantine the Great** until 452 AD, when **Attila the Hun** demolished much of the city, a job the **Goths** finished in 539. In 1162, the city yielded to **Frederick I Barbarossa,** who brought Milan back into his Holy Roman Empire until his defeat at the **Battle of Legnano** in 1176. In 1450, **Francesco Sforza** seized the city and founded a new dynasty, which saw the introduction of the silk industry during the golden Italian Renaissance. **Louis XII** of France seized Milan until 1513, when **Massimiliano Sforza**, with Swiss assistance, reclaimed the city for his family. **Francis I** took it back for France, but a 1529 peace treaty gave the city back to the Sforzas. With the surprising death of the incumbent duke, Milan fell to Hapsburg emperor **Charles V,** who gave the duchy to his son, **Philip II** of Spain. **Napoleon Bonaparte's** arrival in 1796 was embraced by the day's great thinkers, and in 1805, Milan became the capital of the Kingdom of Italy under the French Empire. Austrian rule was reinstated in 1814, after the collapse of the Napoleonic Empire. In 1848, the Milanese people rose up against Austria, continuing their resistance until the second **War of Italian Independence**, when Napoleon III and Victor Emmanuel II arrived.

Milan now occupies 344 square miles (890 square kilometers) in the center of the Po Basin, which lies in the great plain separating the Ticino and Adda rivers. Lying on the border between fertile, swampy plains to the south and arid lands that spread north to the Alps, it sits directly in the center of all the **Val Padana's** traffic routes. Milan is a great manufacturing center, focusing on the mechanical industries, producing automobiles, airplanes, electric appliances and railroad materials.

Milan, circa 1851.

The current capital and chief industrial center of **Belarus**, **Minsk** maintains a steady economy from manufacturing trucks, tractors, electric motors, machine tools, radios, televisions, textiles, and foodstuffs.

Ethnically Russian, Minsk and Belarus (Byelorussia, or White Russian) were alternately Lithuanian or Polish before becoming part of the Tsarist **Russian Empire** in 1793. Minsk was on the front line of Russian defenses against outside aggressors, which included **Napoleon Bonaparte's** 1812 incursion and the German invasion in **World War I**. The **Bolsheviks** overthrew the Tsar in 1917 and established Minsk as the capital of the new **Byelorussian Soviet Socialist Republic (SSR)** in 1919. During **World War II**, Minsk was again under German occupation from 1941 to 1944, during which time the city's large Jewish community was systematically massacred. In 1990, when the Soviet Union ceased to exist, the Byelorussian SSR became the independent nation of Belarus, with its capital still Minsk. The following year, when several former republics of the Soviet Union joined in a loose economic union called the **Commonwealth of Independent States (CIS)**, Belarus became a member and Minsk was chosen over **Moscow** as the headquarters of the new CIS.

Minsk grew faster than any other Soviet city during the last half of the twentieth century, reaching a population of 1.7 million by the 1990s. It has been nearly entirely rebuilt since World War II's destruction. Many parks and skyscraping apartment buildings have grown up along spacious new boulevards, although early Soviet-style buildings remain, including the grand **Mariinsky Cathedral** and the **Bernadine monastery**.

Beside them, on the rolling hills along the **Svisloch River**, Minsk has founded a music conservatory, a palace of winter sports and a number of theaters, enhancing its reputation as a cultural center. The **Academy of Sciences** (1921) and the **Belarus State Theatre of Opera and Ballet** add a major intellectual and educational element to the city's position as leader of the nation.

The Church of St. Simon and St. Helen in Independence (Nezalezhnost') Square, Minsk.

61. MONTREAL, CANADA
Founded in 1642

Montreal is the second largest French-speaking city in the world, as its population is about two-thirds French-speaking. It is, however, spiced minorities of Irish, Chinese, Scottish, West Indian and English-speaking Canadians, who add intensely to the city's cosmopolitan popularity. It is also the major seaport for trade vessels travelling between the Atlantic Ocean and the Great Lakes via the **St. Lawrence River**. Montreal is heralded as one of North America's most cosmopolitan cities, equal to San Francisco and New York in style, financial power and prestige.

Founded in 1642 by French colonists on the island where the St. Lawrence meets the **Ottawa River**, the city was granted its first civic charter by **King Louis XIV** in 1644. For centuries, it grew around a booming fur trade and the industries of wood and leather fabricating, soapmaking and brewing. The long-standing rivalry and conflict between the French and British in North America came to a head in the **French & Indian War** (1756-1763), and in 1760, the city of Montreal surrendered to British forces. During the early nineteenth century, Montreal grew quickly. **John Molson** linked Montreal and Quebec with the first Canadian steamship (1809) and built the city's first magnificent theater (1825). **The Bank of Montreal** (1817) was **Canada's** first, and **McGill University** (1820) followed. From 1844 to 1849, Montreal was the capital of Canada, a reign that ended when a Montreal mob burned down the Parliament building. In 1861, the city's first horse-drawn tramways began operation. The **National Hockey League** (1917) was formed here, and in 1974, **Concordia University** opened for instruction in English.

In 1990, Montreal had a population of 3.1 million, up from 217,000 in 1890. Within those years, Montreal underwent enormous changes, creating a modern metropolis, although **Old Montreal** (Vieux-Montreal) still exists. Today, partly because of the city's preparation for the **International World Exposition** (**Expo 67**) in 1967 and the 1976 **Olympic Games**, Montreal has seen a vast modernization, including the building of the Metro, a subway serving the entire metro area, linking the region's commercial, culinary and artistic life.

The skyline of Montreal.

Moscow, the capital of **Russia** and the **Soviet Union** before it, has long been a pivotal city in the geographically largest country on Earth. The stronghold of the dukes of **Muscovy**, Moscow was home to **Ivan IV (Ivan the Terrible)**, who is credited with founding Russia in the late sixteenth century. **Tsar Peter I (Peter the Great)** established Russia's capital in **St. Petersburg** in 1703, but after the 1917 overthrow of the Russian monarchy and the 1922 creation of the Soviet Union, Moscow was made the capital of both the Soviet Union and the **Russian Federated Soviet Socialist Republic** within it. With the collapse of the Soviet Union in 1991, Moscow remained the capital of the new Russian Republic.

Moscow contains internationally renowned cultural centers as well as ballet and theater troupes. It was also the host city of the **Olympic Games** in 1980. Under both the Tsars and the Soviets, Russia had an extremely centralized government and economy, so Moscow is also very much the economic and political center of Russia. The twentieth century has seen Moscow's population grow from 753,000 to over 8.7 million.

Like St. Petersburg, Moscow has preserved striking examples of Russian baroque architecture, such as the fifteenth century **Kremlin**, which, from its site overlooking the **Neva River**, was the city's first centralized fortress as well as the long-time center of its national government. Two of the city's most popular tourist attractions include the **Cathedral of the Assumption** (1475-1479), with its five golden domes, and the sixteenth century bell tower of Ivan the Great.

Moscow covers 379 square miles (981 square kilometers), which can be viewed in ever widening concentric circles radiating outward from the mighty Kremlin. The **Kitai-Gorod** is comprised by the Kremlin, a half circle of museums and palaces, and more recently, several grand hotels and apartment buildings. To the Kremlin's east lies **Red Square**. On its southern end sits **St. Basil's Cathedral** (1554-1560), which is graced by ten famous domes of differing styles and colors.

Around this hub, Moscow's **Garden Ring** features examples from all of Russian architecture: baroque church architecture, classical buildings, like the old university and the **Lenin State Library**, as well as modern, functional buildings from the 1920s. Around the Garden Ring, outer Moscow's factories and standardized highrises continue to expand. Beyond the newest suburban areas, open land and forest are still accessible within the city's Ring Road.

St. Basil's Cathedral at Red Square, Moscow.

63. MUNICH (MÜNCHEN), GERMANY Founded in 1157

Munich, the capital and largest city of **Bavaria**, **Germany's** largest state, was founded as a simple marketplace for the monks of the eighth century Benedictine Monastery at Tegernsee. The **Wittelsbach** family arrived in 1255 and remained to build the city of Munich and support its artists and architects. Capital of Bavaria since 1504, Munich evolved as a major city after 1825, during the reign of **King Ludwig I**, who commissioned artists, built museums and created parks and boulevards.

Since the thirteenth and fourteenth centuries, Bavaria has been Europe's leading beer-producing region — thanks to cold winters that are more conducive to barley and hops than grapes — and Munich has been the Bavarian brewing industry's center. **Duke Wilhelm IV** decreed the **Reiheitsgebot** (1516), the purity law for beer that is still followed in Germany and elsewhere. Duke Wilhelm was also a great patron of the arts. His son, **Duke Albrecht V**, established Munich's famous court orchestra and amassed an art collection that remains the base of the nation's collection.

The **Thirty Years' War** (1618-1648), fought between European Catholics and Protestants, devastated the city under **Maximilian I,** who was the first leader of the Catholic League (1609). Maximilian went on to grace the city with one of its finest Renaissance wonders, **The Residenz**, the main Imperial Palace. Maximilian II attempted two great palaces, but saw the completion of only the exquisite **Nymphenburg**.

Munich's old city walls no longer exist, although a boulevard rings the city where the walls stood, and six original gates remain. Also remaining is the **Church of Our Lady**, notable because it was built entirely by the people, with no imperial support. Begun in 1468, the massive 325-foot-long (99-meter-long) church was nearly complete in twenty years. The same strength of purpose guided

Ludwig II, who, in the late nineteenth century, supported composer **Richard Wagner**, making Munich once again a champion city of music and stage.

Munich's history was also touched by the **National Socialist (Nazi)** Party, which was born here after Germany's defeat in **World War I** and brought about the collapse of Bavaria's monarchy. **Adolf Hitler**, one of a generation of disaffected political radicals, joined the party in 1919, took it over in 1921, and attempted a violent overthrow of the Bavarian government in November 1923. He was arrested the next day and wrote his book, *Mein Kampf (My Struggle)*, while in prison. Hitler returned to the party, was elected chancellor of Germany in 1933 and ultimately led the nation to defeat in **World War II**.

Since World War II, Munich has continued to uphold her reputation for art and music with the **Bavarian State Opera Company** and the **Munich Philharmonic**. The site of the 1972 **Olympic Games**, Munich is Germany's third largest city, with a 1990 population of 1.2 million, up from 348,000 in 1890.

A street scene in Munich.

Nairobi originated as a railway settlement, and when the railhead arrived in 1899, it was made the capital of the **Ukamba Province**. By 1905, Nairobi had become the capital of the **British East Africa Protectorate**, and remained as **Kenya's** capital when the nation was granted independence in 1963. Throughout the twentieth century, it has been called everything from "one of the nastiest capitals in the world: dirty, dusty, squalid and at the same time pretentious" by Elspeth Huxley, to charming: As W.S. Rainsford said, "Nairobi roses bloom nine months of the year. Roses, passion flowers, pomegranates, orange trees, Bougainvilleas, and much more, make scores of cheap little houses seem bowers of delight."

In the once-wild, south-central part of the country, immigrants from rural Kenya have made Nairobi one of tropical Africa's largest cities. It covers 266 square miles (689 square kilometers) and supports a population of 1.2 million. Five miles south of Nairobi, **Nairobi National Park** (1946) covers 45 square miles (117 square kilometers). Hundreds of bird species share the rolling plains and thick woods with lions, gazelles, rhinoceroses, giraffes, antelopes, zebras, and numerous reptiles. Even the **Government House** was a host to Kenya's animal kingdom in the 1920s: "My love of wild nature failed me for a moment when we were staying there and a half-grown lioness bounded into the room....The Governor was absolutely without fear, and had a wonderful gift for handling wild animals: he would stroke the leopards growling uneasily on their chains...."

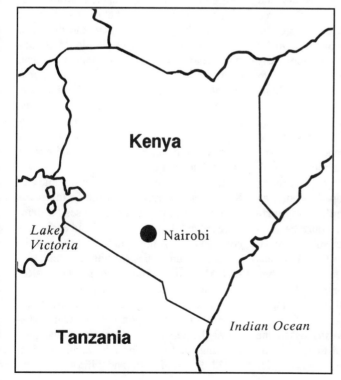

Nairobi is now its country's principal industrial center, with enterprises that include light manufacturing, food processing and beverage and cigarette production. The city also remains the hub for the east African community's railways, harbors and airway corporations.

The city has several fine secondary institutions, including the **University of Nairobi** (1956), the **Kenya Polytechnic** (1961) and the **Kenya Institute of Administration** (1961). Nairobi also houses the **National Museum of Kenya**, the **McMillan Memorial Library** and the **Kenya National Theatre**.

Naples is southern Italy's, if not all Italy's, leading port city. With a population of 1.2 million people, it is Italy's third largest city. By contrast, in 1890, when it was Italy's largest city, it had a population of 463,000. Although Naples is a beautiful city with an invaluable collection of Greek and Roman riches and a history of early Greek elegance (as mentioned in Virgil's *Aeneid*), it does not have the opulence of Rome or Venice. Its priceless charms are in its neapolitan cuisine, hidden alcoves and quiet avenues, rather than in grand plazas.

Naples began as a Greek settlement, **Neopolis** (New City), and retained its Greek language and culture for many years after the Romans took the city in 326 BC. It became a great retreat for Romans, who relaxed in its baths and enjoyed its temples and arenas.

After the fall of the empire, Naples established a republic in the eighth century and fought to retain its independence for three centuries. **Lombardi** forces conquered the city and were subsequently overthrown by the **Normans** in the twelfth century. The **Spanish Hapsburgs** presided from 1503 to 1734, the year that the French **Bourbons** made Naples the capital of a great independent southern kingdom. **Napoleon** arrived in 1798, declaring a republic, which scattered the royal family to Palermo and abroad. The **Parthenopean Republic** was born, although in 1799 the **Bourbons** returned, executing the republicans, who had hoped to build an independent paradise. **Joseph Bonaparte** came in 1805, chasing the court back to Palermo, and this time French rule remained until the fall of Napoleon. The Austrians then helped return Naples to the Bourbon monarch, who maintained control until 1860, when **Giuseppe Garibaldi** made Naples part of a united Italy.

Located between **Mt. Vesuvius** to the east and the volcanic **Campi Flegrei** to the northwest, Naples sits on 62 square miles

The Piazza Plebiscito in Naples, circa 1930.

(160 square kilometers) of land amongst the hills arcing around the **Bay of Naples**, which is still southern Italy's principal port, although its importance has been declining alongside the city's.

The Gothic church of **San Lorenzo Maggiore** stands over ancient Roman remains that are now sheltered within its walls, as the great **Boccaccio** and **Petrarch** were sheltered, and **San Paolo Maggiore** stands atop the site of an ancient Roman temple. Its exterior is adorned with the fossils of Greek and Roman art. **The Duomo**, dedicated to the patron saint **Januarius**, holds a chapel of antique columns, paintings and sculpture. Excavations under its foundation have exposed the outlines of Naples' ancient center.

The vast church within the complex of **Santa Chiara**, erected for the **Franciscans** in the fourteenth century, houses "a damaged splendor of royal tombs and early frescoes." Naples is home to two of the world's finest museums, the **National Archaeological Museum,** which features Greco-Roman masterpieces in marble, bronze, mosaic and ceramic, and the **National Museum de Gallery of Capodimonte**, which displays the tapestries, porcelain works and paintings of Italian masters, including **Botticelli, Parmigianino** and **Titian**.

New Orleans was founded as the capital of French **Louisiana**, which once stretched all the way to Canada. New Orleans is a unique city, whose culture — as well as its celebrated cuisine — is flavored by its French origins, by Afro-Caribbean (**Creole**) influences and by the Acadian (**Cajun**) culture, which took root during the nineteenth century in the remote southern Louisiana and **Mississippi River** Delta areas.

Because of its location as a virtual island in the bayou country of the Mississippi Delta, New Orleans developed independently from the rest of Louisiana until the 1930s, when connecting highways were built.

New Orleans' population, which is divided almost equally between blacks and whites, grew in the twentieth century from 242,000 to 500,000. The city has always been Louisiana's largest, today covering an area of 364 square miles (943 square kilometers). New Orleans has also always been a port town. It is America's second largest port in terms of tonnage handled, thanks to its excellent position on the Mississippi River between **Lake Pontchartrain** and the **Gulf of Mexico**. The city was built primarily on the east bank of a sharp bend in the Mississippi, and there it grew into a commercial center around the busy harbor, exporting agricultural products, chemicals, textiles, oils and tobacco, as well as acting as a major grain port worldwide. The city's economy is stable and rich, but oil rig fires, mercury, arsenic and lead discharges have been a continual threat to the city's drinking water.

Water has always been one of the city's main problems because for New Orleans, it is inescapable. Due to the mighty Mississippi, hurricanes and drainage problems, which are caused by elevations as low as five feet below sea level, the city fears that it may lose some of its oldest, most charming districts to the encroaching waters.

Home of the annual **Mardi Gras** festival, for which Americans and foreign guests travel great distances, its culture is also one of the nation's most unusual. With its famous reputation as the birthplace of **jazz**, its history of powerful **voodoo sects**, its impressive Old World, French architecture on the **Vieux Carre** (Old Square) and its **French Quarter,** where **Creole** architecture is seen in one-story cottages with windows that are built from the floor up and open directly onto the sidewalks, the city is extremely colorful and engaging. Its streets are always full of great poets, talented musicians, general pleasure seekers and skilled handcraftsmen.

A classic scene at the Jackson Square levee, New Orleans.

As America's largest and arguably greatest city (and also in competition for the world's greatest city), **New York City** has never lost its mysterious energy that brought — and continues to bring — immigrants to its streets from every nation of the world.

The Dutch navigator **Henry Hudson** arrived in 1609. Five years later, his countryman, **Peter Minuit**, bought **Manhattan Island**, the present city's centerpiece, from Native Americans, establishing the settlement of **New Amsterdam**. This city was sold in 1664 to Britain's **Duke of York**, who renamed it New York. After the **American Revolution**, **George Washington** was inaugurated as the first president of the United States here, and the **United States Congress** met here from 1785 to 1790. At the end of the nineteenth century, New York was expanded from just Manhattan (then with a population of 1.5 million) to include its adjacent cities, which became its boroughs. These are the mostly-rural **Staten Island**, the **Bronx**, which is on the **New York State** mainland, and two on **Long Island**: **Queens** and **Brooklyn**, which, after Manhattan, is the most populous, with 806,000 people. Today, the five boroughs' combined population is 7.3 million.

Its mystique has made New York the world's best known commercial metropolis and the nation's romantic center of culture, liberty and intellectualism. It's impossible to sum up the city's overwhelming personality, evidenced in its monstrous skyscrapers, its overcrowded streets, its non-stop entertainment districts and its people — pop artists, corporate moguls and literati. Its street names have literally become synonyms for aspects of American culture: **Wall Street** for finance, **Broadway** for theater, **Fifth Avenue** for high-end retail, **Madison Avenue** for the myths

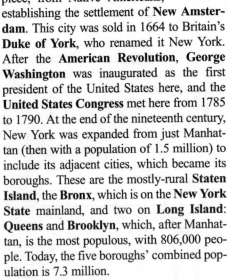

The Statue of Liberty.

and dreams of advertising, **Seventh Avenue** for fashion, **SoHo** (South of **Houston Street**) for contemporary fine art, and so on.

The **Statue of Liberty** was installed here, at the city's feet, to welcome the tides of Irish, Italian, Asian, Jewish, and Puerto Rican immigrants. All the nation's finest artists, writers, actors, journalists and musicians have graced New York, or have been graced by it. **V.S. Pritchett** wrote, "If Paris suggests intelligence, if London suggests experience, then the word for New York is activity," and the city's character remains the same.

The city reached its apogee in the 1940s and 1950s, when, as an American symbol, it attracted the cream of European society. At the end of **World War II**, New York City was a natural choice for the **United Nation's** headquarters, as it already had been for most major American corporations since the nineteenth century. By the 1960s, however, high taxes and extreme crime dulled New York's image, compelling most of the corporate headquarters to relocate elsewhere. Yet attendance at the city's great museums, which include the **Metropolitan Museum of Art**, the **Museum of Modern Art (MOMA)** and the **American Museum of Natural History**, is up, and the nation's largest publishers are still based here, though their numbers have dwindled considerably. Its excellent schools, like **Columbia University**, **New York University** and the **Julliard School of Music**, are still world-renowned. The city's romantic theater district, located around **Times Square** on Broadway, is regaining its reputation, while **off-Broadway** and **off off-Broadway** shows experiment with avant-garde styles. **Carnegie Hall** still hosts the world's finest musicians, and the artistic districts of **SoHo** and **Greenwich Village** still attract young artists.

It is said that Tokyo is **Japan's** political center, while **Osaka** is its commercial center. Boasting that their city does 40 percent of Japan's business, Osaka's populace once took great pride in the grey smokey air that hung around its industrialized area, earning it the name "the capital of smoke." Since the 1970s, however, the citizens of Osaka have become increasingly concerned about pollution, so a campaign to increase air and water quality has been under way since the 1980s. Osaka has also been called "the Chicago of Japan" for its industry and "the Venice of Japan" for its seventy canals and over 1,000 bridges.

The city spans 495 square miles (1,282 square kilometers) of a basin made by the **Ikoma Mountains** to the east, the **Izumi Mountains** in the south and the **Rokko Mountains** in the northwest. It is also now linked with the city of **Kobe**, forming a megapolis. Osaka's streets are arranged in a grid formation. The central business district in Osaka's northern section holds an island, located on the **Yodo River**, that contains **City Hall**, the **Central Civic Hall**, the **Bank of Japan** and the **Asahi Press** headquarters. The city's two traditional commercial centers, **Semba** and **Shimanouchi Streets**, existed for centuries until bombing in **World War II** demolished their old world shops and hidden family quarters.

Shards of pottery have identified Osaka as a site inhabited as early as the Paleolithic Age. **Ancient burial grounds** underlie the plain on which the city was built, and the largest tomb of the **Tumulus period**, ascribed to **Emperor Nintoku**, is a fifth century structure fortified by three moats and covering some 80 acres. In 1496, **Rennyo**, a militant priest of the True Pure Land sect of **Buddhism**, built a fortress temple. Completed in 1532, it was destroyed, along with the surrounding town, by **Oda Nobunaga** in 1580. Nobunaga's successor, **Toyotomi Hideyoshi**, then employed over 30,000 workers to build the great **Hideyoshi Castle** and its massive stone walls. Around this castle developed the infant town of present-day Osaka, which was the seat of national power until Hideyoshi's death in 1598.

Osaka became a center for the cultural renaissance of the **Genroku period** (seventeenth and eighteenth centuries), when new dramatic forms like the **Bunraku** and **Kabuki Theatre** were created. The city experienced a serious setback in 1837, when the Tokugawa shogun **Ieyushi** spawned a massive riot during Japan's great famine by refusing to open Osaka's storehouses to the starving populace, who then burned forty percent of Osaka to the ground. The city was repaired, and in 1871, the government opened its first postal run between Tokyo and Osaka. Growth picked up and continued throughout the nineteenth and twentieth centuries, swelling the population to 2.6 million in 1990.

Osaka has over 100 junior colleges and universities, including **Osaka University, Osaka University of Foreign Studies** and **Osaka University of Education**, as well as a blooming tradition of modern Japanese drama and music. The city also features a lively collection of nightclubs that offer excellent jazz and other Western style performances. The city's atmosphere and industry made it the site of both the 1970 and 1990 **World Fairs.**

The neighboring city of Kobe suffered a massive earthquake in early 1995, killing 3,000 and reaping severe damage. While Osaka also was physically injured in the earthquake, the long-term inactivity of Kobe's port will have a more serious economic impact on the city.

Osaka Castle.

Oslo, Norway's capital and largest city, is an excellent center for trade, culture and outdoor amusements. The original city was destroyed by fire in 1624 and rebuilt by **Christian IV** of Denmark as **Christiania**. The city remained small, with fewer than 100,000 citizens, until the late nineteenth century, when its excellent harbor was employed for free trade, a telegraph network was developed and a great railway expansion, continuing into the last half of the twentieth century, linked Oslo's industrial wealth with remote areas of Norway.

Much of Oslo's success is due to its superb geographic location. Sitting at the head of a fjord on a natural harbor, Oslo bridges two of its nation's most important counties, **Ostfold** and **Vestfold** (home of the first kings of Norway), which have the largest concentration of both good farmland and industry. Between them, Oslo has developed as their cultural, industrial and financial link. Covering an area of 175 square miles (454 square kilometers), with a metropolitan population of only about a half-million, much of the city's lands are covered by protected virgin forests and well-stocked lakes, providing a great deal of outdoor recreation.

Each March, **Holmenkollen** holds the world's biggest ski meet, drawing more than 100,000 spectators, including the Royal Family of Norway. Oslo was the site of the 1952 **Olympic Games**, and Norway's current king was a 1957 Olympic winner.

Oslo also has a history of producing fine artists. **Frogner Park** was built to feature over 150 sculptures by **Gustav Vigeland**. The **Munch Museum** (1963) rotates its enormous collection — composed of 1,000 paintings and 4,473 drawings and watercolors, as well as several sculptures — of expressionist **Edvard Munch's** work.

Evidence of the **Viking tradition** has been preserved in many local museums. The **Norwegian Folk Museum** at Bygdoy features three restored Viking ships, while the **Framhuset** houses the original **Fram**, the vessel used by **Fridtjof Nansen** and **Roald Amundsen** in their polar exploration.

Though the architecture of Oslo is generally solid, simple and fairly new, **Akershus Castle**, built in the late thirteenth century, still stands on its perch, overlooking the harbor. Along with the functional docks that crowd the harbor's banks, Oslo's seaside location has created a hearty population of explorers and sports-loving men and women who retain the adventurous character of their hearty Viking ancestors.

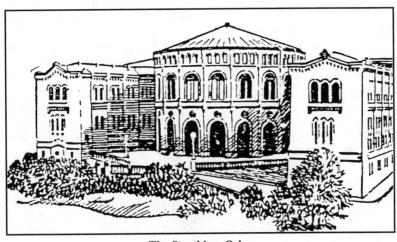

The Storthing, Oslo.

Paris, France's capital and largest city, would top any list of the world's greatest cities. Contemporary Paris is more united than in older days, when the **Left Bank** of the **Seine** was famous for its artists, the **Right Bank** was the city's economic center and the **central city** was the seat of religious

The Arc de Triomphe, Paris.

authority. Greater Paris currently covers an area of 890 square miles (1,118 square kilometers) and houses a population of 2.1 million (10.7 million in the Parisian region).

Paris has been the fertile earth for many of the world's most inventive and talented painters, including **Henri de Toulouse-Lautrec, Jean Edouard Vuillard, Paul Gauguin**, and the Impressionists **Edgar Degas** and **Claude Monet**. The city has housed generations of immortalized writers, like **Honoré de Balzac, George Sand, Gertrude Stein, Ernest Hemingway, Henry Miller** and **Colette**, as well as great thinkers, who often meet in the famous cafés of the **Champs-Elysees**. Paris has also preserved some of the world's greatest works of art. The **Louvre's** collection includes the **Venus de Milo**, the **Mona Lisa** and the **Victory of Samothrace** and spans from the seventh century BC to the mid-nineteenth century. The world-renowned museum occupies four sides of an exquisite palace surrounding the **Cour Carree** (Square Court), where Vikings first camped in 885 during their unsuccessful siege of Paris.

Among the city's world-class treasures are the cathedral of **Notre Dame de Paris**, which was the site of the Gallo-Roman altar to Jupiter before Christianity as well as **Napoleon Bonaparte's** crowning as em-

peror in 1804, the **Saint-Chapel**, which was built with stained glass walls to house the crown of thorns worn by Christ, the **Eiffel Tower** (1889), which is the indisputable symbol of the Paris skyline, and the **Arc de Triomphe**.

The city has been considered important since the first century BC, when ancient Paris (called **Lutetia**) was made the capital of the **Parissi** tribe. When the Romans arrived, **Caesar** wrote that the Gallic tribe burned their town rather than surrender it to the empire.

Under the monarchs of the **House of Bourbon** that ruled France from 1589 to 1792, Paris became the center of a global empire and attained its position as one of the world's most glamorous cities. The **French Revolution** (1789) brought down the Bourbons, who were ultimately replaced by Napoleon Bonaparte, who brought only temporary glory to France, but added permanently to Paris' mystique.

Napoleon III enlisted **Baron Haussmann** as city planner for the overpopulated, industrialized Paris of the late nineteenth century, and his works were extremely popular through the **Franco-Prussian War** (1870-1871) and the French Commune. Paris was the site of the **World's Fair** in 1889 and the **Olympic Games** in 1900, and again in 1924.

For such a grand city, Paris still faces the common challenges of vast urban development, like a high unemployment rate and a volatile populace, which erupted into violent protest in 1968. However, the city of Paris retains its title as "the City of Light" and continues to attract bright national and international citizens.

Philadelphia, whose population reached 1.6 million in 1990, was one of North America's earliest major metropolises and once **New York City's** active rival. The city's 471 square mile area (1,182 square kilometers), America's fourth largest, still reflects the Quaker and colonial styles that defined the city's character in the seventeenth and eighteenth centuries. Philadelphia was founded in 1681 by **William Markham**. His cousin, the young idealist **William Penn**, designed the city, which was the first in America to be laid out in a grid. Penn named the city after "brotherly love," envisioning a city that would remain forever green and devoted to Quaker ideals.

Some of his dreams were realized. Philadelphia was long reputed to be one of the nation's most tolerant cities, admitting Roman Catholics and Jewish immigrants when no other English colony would, and supporting powerful black communities that fought slavery, hid escaped slaves and worked for freedom and civil liberties before the **Civil War**. In the 1960s, Philadelphia suffered the same racial tensions as other American cities, but has emerged with a healthy black community of wealthy and middle class citizens.

It is said that Philadelphians are great joiners, which has led to a city of easily-engaged citizens that work hard for their communities' success. This same spirit led to an early industrial prosperity. Philadelphia took raw iron from inland furnaces and built the first American-built steam locomotives. The city also excelled in textile manufacturing and shipbuilding, leather working, sugar refining and the production of other supplies that supported the Union during the Civil War.

The city, which was the site of both the **First Continental Congress** in 1774 and the **Second Continental Congress** in 1775, was named the capital of the United States in 1790, three years after the **Constitutional Convention** met there and the **Constitution** was framed. The city's pride is evidenced by the official certification of 7,500 buildings, some dating back to 1643, as landmarks to be preserved. These include structures in some of the city's oldest sections, such as the **Southwark, Society Hill** and **Independence Hall** areas. Both the **Liberty Bell Pavilion** and Independence Hall are contained in **Independence National Historical Park** (1956). Philadelphia still has more park land than any other American city, and **Fairmount Park** (used for the **Centennial Exposition of 1876**) remains the nation's largest landscaped park.

The oldest continually inhabited street in the nation is Philadelphia's **Elfreth's Alley**. Benjamin Franklin opened the nation's first free library, the nation's first hospital and the **American Philosophical Society** in Philadelphia. The city was the nation's first theatrical center, drawing the European talent that was later attracted to New York. It was also the country's first financial center and the heart of the country's banking system, until New York overtook that title in the 1850s.

Independence Hall, Philadelphia.

First mentioned in 310 BC as **Campania**, it is believed that **Pompeii's** original settlement may date back to the eighth century BC. The city became a "time capsule" on August 24, 79 AD, when its nearby volcano, **Mount Vesuvius**, erupted, blanketing the city with suffocating ash and lava.

A thriving city before the eruption, Pompeii now exists as an excellent example of everyday life in the ancient **Roman Empire** of the first century. When Vesuvius exploded without warning, bakers were tending loaves in ovens that were in full operation, families were collaborating on projects and merchants were selling their wares. The force was so wild and surprising that Pompeii's thousands of citizens had no time to prepare. They were caught under the flow and remained there, undiscovered and untouched until 1748.

The city was built originally on a prehistoric lava flow north of the **Sarnus River's** mouth. The town's southwestern section was the oldest, and two miles of wall enclosed about 155 acres (63 hectares). Seven city gates have been excavated, along with numerous public buildings that were found in three major groups. The first group is the **Forum** in the southwest, where religious, economic and municipal powers were centered. One great pagan temple was dedicated to the deities Jupiter, Juno and Minerva. A market lay to the east, and the sanctuary of the city's guardian deities to the south. The **Patroness Eumachia's** woolen industry headquarters were also in the Forum section of the city.

The **Triangular Forum**, the second of the three sections, was the site of a theater, **The Doric Temple**, which is the cities' oldest, and the temples of **Zeus and Isis**.

The **Amphitheater**, the oldest ever discovered, was built after the Roman colony was established at Pompeii. This comprises the third section. Along with these three meeting places, baths, luxurious homes from 200 BC, and great mosaics were found throughout the city. Excavation continues today, informing us of religion's great role in ancient Rome and the techniques used for everything from baking to city planning. Each new discovery continues to affect our view of Roman life the same way that Pompeii's first discovery inspired Europeans to adapt aspects of Roman life and culture to their own.

The remains of Pompeii.

Called "the city of 100 spires" for its preserved buildings of Gothic, baroque, rococo and classical architecture, the **Czech Republic's** capital, currently home to 1.2 million, is one of Europe's finest, most beautiful cities. **Prague** has long been recognized for its cultural life, populated throughout its history by characters such as **Wolfgang Amadeus Mozart**, who first performed his **Prague Symphony** and **Don Giovanni** here, the great Czech composers **Bedrich Smetana** and **Antonin Dvorak**, the physicist **Albert Einstein**, seventeenth century astronomers **Tycho Brahe** and **Johannes Kepler** and the twentieth century thespian-turned-president, **Vaclav Havel**.

Prague was the capital of **Bohemia**, a kingdom that was part of the Austro-Hungarian Empire. When the independent Republic of Czechoslovakia was established in 1918, Prague was the capital, and when the country divided into the **Slovak Republic** and the **Czech Republic** in 1992, Prague remained the latter's capital.

Along with great architects, Prague has been host to some of Europe's great leaders. Though the **Reformation** put men like scholar **Jan Hus** to death, and popular revolutions were often violent, desperate attempts, **Jan Zizka** was able to organize peasant rebels, who joined with **Hussites**, to win Prague back from the Roman Catholic **King Sigismund** in the fifteenth century. In 1526, the Roman Catholic **Hapsburgs** captured Bohemia and returned to Prague, where a second battle with the **Protestants** ended in their defeat, enhancing the tensions that would bring on the **Thirty Years' War**.

In 1968, attempts to reform the strict Communist regime, which was installed by the Soviets at the end of **World War II**, led to "the Prague Spring" that promised a new form of Communism under **Alexander Dubcek**. However, Warsaw Pact troops moved in and reestablished a censorious, oppressive and centralized government. In 1989, Vaclav Havel led the citizens of Prague against this repressive leadership in the "Velvet Revolution," which insisted on democracy. The Communist government resigned, and Havel became president.

Prague's metropolitan area covers 192 square miles (496 square kilometers). Its inner core of historic buildings, bridges and residences has remained remarkably well preserved and unchanged over the past two centuries. Theaters and museums flourish alongside some of Europe's most treasured churches. The Romanesque **Church of St. George** survives from the tenth century, as does the twin-spired **St. Vitus Cathedral**. Europe's oldest Jewish cemetery exists here, as do the great **Valdstein** and **Clam-Gallas Palaces**, two of Prague's excellent baroque treasures. Prague's history as a cultural center is particularly evident during its annual spring music festival that features the **Prague Symphony** and the **Czech Philharmonic** and draws guests from all over Europe and the world.

A panoramic view of Prague.

Stretching from **Sugar Loaf Mountain** to the glistening beaches of the Atlantic Ocean, over the gentle **Serra do Mar Mountains**, north to the wild **Brazilian jungles**, the city of Rio de Janeiro inhabits one of the loveliest spots on Earth. The name, meaning "River of January," was given to the city because Portuguese navigators mistook the bay they discovered for the mouth of a river. As the capital of Brazil from 1822 to 1960, (the year Brasilia was built in the jungle), and the capital of Rio de Janeiro state currently, the city has gained and maintained an international popularity. Its beaches are world-famous. Its yearly **Carnival** draws international revelers, and its economic success began with the decadence of the sugar, diamond and gold trade. The city has grown into both a luscious resort for visitors and a serious cultural capital, featuring institutions like the **Brazilian Academy of Letters, the Brazilian Academy of Sciences, the National Historical Museum** and the **National Museum**, which took up residence in the former **Imperial Palace**.

The city, covering a total of 452 square miles (673 square kilometers), is sometimes called two cities because the exotic **South Zone**, set apart by the mild mountain range behind it, is connected to the city of Rio only by three tunnels running through the granite. The South Zone, known for the leisurely pace of its sun-worshiping populace, is a very narrow stretch, just large enough for the retirement homes and apartments between beach and rock.

North and west of **Mount Corcovado**, from which one can see both cities, Rio has grown into a modern metropolis. Its port at **Guanabara Bay** was expanded in 1807, when **Napoleon** drove **Prince Regent Dom Joao** and 10,000 members of the Portuguese court into Brazil, where Rio became the de facto capital of the entire **Portuguese Empire**. In 1820, **Dom Pedro** declared Brazil free from Portuguese rule and named himself emperor. Coffee, cotton and rubber trades were expanded and the city saw a quick expansion. Steamboat operations began in 1835, and in 1868 the first tramcars succeeded the horse-drawn buses. Currently, Rio, with its skyscrapers and its multinational corporations, is governed by a mayor.

Rio is known not just for its beaches, but the extravagance and ceremony of the nine million people who inhabit its metropolitan area. When the Portuguese came in 1560 to expel the French, their population was so limited that interracial relations became common. A great mix of **Roman Catholicism** and "**Macumba**" spiritualism has colored the character of Rio.

An aerial view of Rio de Janeiro.

According to legend, the city of Rome was founded by twins, **Romulus** and **Remus**, who were raised by a she-wolf. Romulus killed his brother in anger and lived to be named a god. The city is named after him, and is built on the banks of the **Tiber River**, seated in and on top of the most awe-inspiring historical remnants in all of Europe.

Within the city's **Aurelian Wall**, built of brick-faced concrete in 270 AD when the city had outgrown the original **Servian Wall**, built around 380 BC, **Rome's seven hills** and western regions are currently adorned with over 200 palaces, twenty churches, eight fine parks, monuments like **the Pantheon** and the **Roman Coliseum**, the **Roman Forum** and the walled **Vatican City**, as well as the **houses of Parliament**, the residence of the Italian president and around 300 hotels.

Though the walled city constitutes only four percent of the municipality's 582 square miles (1,507 square kilometers), it is home to some of the greatest artistic treasures in the world, including **Michelangelo's ceiling** in Vatican City's **Sistine Chapel**, the architecturally striking **Scalinata della Trinita dei Monti**, known as the Spanish steps, where students, tourists and residents gather at all hours, the **Trevi Fountain**, built in 1932, **Bernini's** bridges and **St. Peter's Basilica**, where Michelangelo's **Pieta** is still on view.

Rome's wealth can be traced through its centuries. Between 375 and 275 BC, Rome gained control of the entire peninsula of Italy and constructed the famous aqueducts that served the city with fresh water. The **War with Carthage**, beginning in 264 BC, lasted more than a century, leaving Rome in control of the **Mediterranean**.

Though in control of a vast empire, Rome was troubled by poverty, an expanded population and housing shortages. **Julius Caesar's** son **Augustus** added baths, theaters, temples and the first fire brigade in 21 BC. **Claudius** began a great port near **Ostia**, and Nero introduced town planning, though the fire destroyed more than he could save. **Hadrian** built the **Pantheon** and his **mausoleum**.

With the beginning of the **Renaissance** in the fifteenth century, scholars and artists were drawn to Rome by the Church, and **Leo X** (1513-1521) supported young Michelangelo and **Raphael**.

Napoleon occupied Rome in 1798, but in 1809 Rome and the Papal States were annexed to France. The **Revolution of 1846-1878** convinced **Pope Pius IX** to become a staunch conservative, and he tried to save the power of the Church with French support.

The **Kingdom of Italy** included most of the Papal States, excluding Rome, which fought off **Garibaldi** in 1862 and 1867. In 1870, France withdrew her support and Rome became the capital of a united Italy. Today, the almost tragic beauty of classical Rome seems to survive in the spirit and history of its 2,831,000 citizens.

The ruins of the Roman Coliseum.

The second largest city in **Missouri**, **Saint Louis** is important to American history as its symbolic "jumping-off" place for westward emigration. The 630-foot (190-meter) **Gateway Arch** that dominates its skyline represents this fact. Established as a fur-trading post on the west bank of the **Mississippi River** by Frenchman **Auguste Chouteau**, the city is named for the French patron saint of King Louis XV. The post was a Spanish possession from 1770 to 1803, when it was ceded back to France and sold to the United States as part of the **Louisiana Purchase**.

Saint Louis remained an important fur-trading center. More important, however, is the city's position at the confluence of the Mississippi and **Missouri rivers** that make it the West's natural gateway. The legendary **Meriwether Lewis** and **William Clark** expedition to the Pacific departed from here in 1804, as did many thousands wagon trains that headed out across the Great Plains to take their place on the **Oregon Trail**, the **California Trail** and the **Santa Fe Trail**.

By the late nineteenth century, Saint Louis had evolved into a major railroad hub and Mississippi River port for the transshipment of grain, livestock and other agricultural products from the American heartland. These activities still form the backbone of the region's economy, although brewing and aircraft manufacturing are now also very important.

In 1904, Saint Louis hosted the glorious **World's Fair** that set the new century's tone. During the twentieth century, Saint Louis' population remained at about 400,000 because many urban residents moved to its outlying suburbs. Meanwhile, the population of Saint Louis' cross-state rival, **Kansas City**, has grown from 133,000 to 453,000.

An aerial view of the Gateway Arch and the city of Saint Louis.

Saint Petersburg, the city founded by **Tsar Peter the Great** in 1703 as the capital of the **Russian Empire**, was his "window on Europe" because of its excellent position as **Russia's** only year-round port. Peter captured Swedish fortresses on the **Neva River** and then fortified the other islands of the river delta. Peter constructed a shipyard on the city's banks and invited noblemen to settle in the new capital. As the city grew, it spread over the many small islands defined by the Neva's tributaries, which empty into the **Gulf of Finland**, which is surrounded by a horseshoe-shaped land mass.

The islands and mainland of St. Petersburg, encompassing 139 square miles (360 square kilometers) are now home to over 4.4 million people, four times its population at the end of the Tsarist era. Saint Petersburg was intended to be an imposing capital inhabited by the cultural elite. Palaces and monuments were built in the mid-eighteenth century, and industry flourished while factory workers lived in impoverished slums.

With their great numbers and a growing dissatisfaction, the workers of Saint Petersburg revolted, failing in 1905 and then succeeding in 1917. After the Revolution, **Moscow** became Russia's capital, and Saint Petersburg was briefly renamed **Petrograd** (Peter's Town). In 1924, upon the death of **Nikolai Lenin**, the leader of the Revolution, the city became **Leningrad**.

The Germans targeted Leningrad for one of the most powerful attacks of **World War II**. The city subsequently suffered shortages and fatalities during the bitter Russian winter. The Germans, after massive fatalities of their own, were driven back in 1944, and Leningrad was given the title "Hero City" for its resistance.

With the collapse of Communism in 1991, Lenin fell out of favor, and, after living so long in his shadow, voters chose to restore the city's original name, Saint Petersburg.

It is now one of the world's most visually striking cities. Grand buildings like the **Winter Palace**, with its baroque excesses, are complimented by museums, state buildings and **St. Isaac's Cathedral**, which were designed in the classical style that reemerged at the end of the eighteenth century. Palaces destroyed by the German attack in World War II have been painstakingly restored to their original beauty, and the first house in Saint Petersburg, built by **Peter the Great** himself in the early 1700s, still stands as a museum.

An early twentieth century view of Saint Petersburg's skyline.

Called the Athens, the Paris and the New York of the West, **San Francisco**, California, evolved from the Spanish **Presidio de San Francisco** and the **Mission of St. Francis of Assisi** (the Mission Dolores), both established in 1776, and the small village of **Yerba Buena** that sprang up on **Yerba Buena Cove** half a century later.

In 1846, as California became a territory of the United States, the American flag was raised in San Francisco. The discovery of gold in 1848 in the foothills of the **Sierra Nevada** launched The great **Gold Rush** of 1849, and by 1851, the quiet village had exploded into one of the most vibrant, cities of the age. The city's cosmopolitan character emerged early. A city of immigrants from the very beginning, San Francisco has been called the only city in the United States with no minorities, because it has no majority. Of the city's 800,000 residents, the melting pot includes first to fourth generation Italians, Japanese, Hispanics Russians and others, with the principal ethnic groups being the Chinese and the Irish.

The 1906 earthquake and fire destroyed much of the heart of San Francisco, but the citizens rebuilt their city to its previous splendor within five years and hosted the **Panama Pacific Exposition** in 1915. The city's history as a financial center is evidenced in the **financial district**, built on reclaimed land from the original **Yerba Buena cove** and the ashes of the 1906 disaster. The business hub was immediately rebuilt with fine and delicate architecture, and the city's new modern giants, like the **Transamerica Pyramid** and the **Bank of America Center**, have helped recreate a Manhattan-like skyline.

In the 1920s and 1930s, the **Twin Peaks tunnel** linked the city to the sand dunes to the west, which became the residential **Sunset** and **Richmond districts**, while the **Bay Bridge** and the **Golden Gate Bridge** opened the city to Oakland in the east and to the Marin headlands to the north. San Francisco grew into a massive banking city because of the gold rush, and a transport city because of the harbor, though it has lost port traffic to other western cites such as **Oakland**.

Masterful legends like **Mark Twain** and **Bret Harte** came to behold the mythical wild city of the West, and in the twentieth century, the **Beat generation** built poetry out of dissatisfaction, idealism and jazz music on the edge of the Italian enclave called **North Beach**, which borders the markets and overcrowded tenements of **Chinatown**. **The Beats** gave rise to the **Hippies**, who "dropped out, turned on and tuned in" on the streets of the **Haight-Ashbury** area, where popular music legends **The Grateful Dead** and **Jefferson Airplane** created a new brand of rock 'n' roll, known as "the San Francisco Sound."

Golden Gate Park, created in the nineteenth century, houses the **California Academy of Sciences**, the **de Young Museum** and the **Japanese Tea Garden**.

San Francisco's skyline as seen from Treasure Island.

Santa Fe, the capital city of New Mexico, is built on one of the oldest settlements in the United States. It was founded in the **Sangre de Cristo Mountains** on the site of an ancient pueblo on the **Santa Fe River** in the north central section of New Mexico, of which it was made the capital in 1912. The Spanish, under New Mexico's governor **Pedro de Peralta**, erected a public square in 1609, and the city's new buildings began to radiate out from this center. Even contemporary buildings tend to maintain the colonial style of early settlers. Santa Fe is still a city of old adobe houses, tiled roofs, narrow streets and shady, old colonial patios. The population, reaching 117,000 in 1990, up from 6,000 in 1890.

Along with the city's unique atmosphere, its old world crafts and ethnic variety, Santa Fe is a cultural and artistic center in the West. The **summer opera season** in Santa Fe is attended by people of all nations, lasting through June and July and featuring excellent standard works, as well as ambitious original pieces. The opera's **open-air theater** was carved out of a mountainside in 1968. The city also acts as a magnet for artists who find inspiration in the city's deep history and setting. The arts and crafts colony began in 1923 and is still the center for artists' gatherings and displays.

To further protect the city's heritage, excavation continues in the old Indian pueblos, and early buildings, like the **Mission of San Miguel of Santa Fe** (1621), thought to be the oldest church in the United States, are maintained rather than demolished for modern building. Also protected is the **Palace of the Governors**, built with massive walls in 1610 on the central plaza, and used for 300 years as the seat of Spanish government, then Mexican, then Confederate, and then Union forces before New Mexico was admitted into the Union in 1912. It is the nation's oldest public building.

A three day festival is still held annually to commemorate the Mexican reconquest of the city in 1692, after it had been abandoned in 1680 to attacking Indian tribes. Soon after, French colonial traders travelled over the now famous **Santa Fe Trail** from Missouri and settled. Mexico obtained its independence from Spain in 1821, and Americans took the city in the **Mexican War** of 1846. New Mexico became the 47th state in 1912, and Santa Fe remained the new state's capital.

The Palace of the Governors dates from the seventeenth century.

In the center of **Chile**, between the **Andes Mountains** to the east and the **Pacific Coastal Range** to the west, **Santiago**, Chile's capital, lies in the fertile **Central Valley**. Founded by the Spanish soldier **Pedro de Valdivia**, who wrested the lands from the **Araucanian Indians** in 1541, Santiago grew slowly as Spanish settlers arrived, set up their wealthy, European styled households and subdued the indigenous population. The city gained greater prominence when it was made the capital in 1818, the year that Chile gained independence.

In 1879, Chile won copper-rich lands from **Bolivia** and **Peru** in the **War of the Pacific**. Santiago then became the industrial and economic center of a mineral-rich empire, producing not only copper, but the necessary nitrates for the Allies' bombs in **World War II**.

The city's beauty is heightened by its enduring economic stability. Though a quarter of Santiago's 4.4 million people are poor, living around the city in shanty towns, many of its remaining residents have a more comfortable, middle- to upper-class lifestyle, living in suburban homes with manicured landscapes. They visit the many shops standing on the **Plaza de Armas**, the heart of downtown Santiago. They walk the tree-lined **Avenida Bernardo O'Higgins**, which is lined with monuments and public buildings. They enjoy the city's **two symphony orchestras, the Museum of Natural History** and the **Biblioteca Nacional**, South America's largest library.

With an area of 128 square miles (331 square kilometers), Santiago is Chile's largest city and its center for banking, its stock exchange and its cultural institutions, like the **Municipal Theatre**, where Santiago's orchestras perform. Santiago also has several higher learning institutions, including the **University of Chile**, the **Catholic University of Chile** and the **Technical University**.

In 1970, Santiago also became a focal point for political change after the election of Marxist President **Salvador Allende**, who vowed to nationalize industry. After being unseated by a military coup in 1973, Allende reportedly "took his own life".

The city recovered a measure of stability, completing its **Metro** subway system in 1980 and continuing construction of public housing and other advancements throughout the 1980s.

Iglesia Cathedral in Santiago.

As Latin America's foremost industrial center and Brazil's largest city, **São Paulo** has been called "the locomotive that pulls the rest of Brazil." As its nation's capital, the city not only leads in the production of goods, such as textiles, electrical appliances, furniture and chemical products, São Paulo also boasts one of the world's fastest growing metropolitan populations. Within its 576 square miles (1,493 square kilometers), São Paulo supports a population of 10.1 million people, compared to a mere 75,000 in 1890. By contrast, São Paulo's chief rival, **Rio de Janeiro,** grew from 500,000 to 5.6 million. São Paulo is projected to be the world's largest city in the twenty-first century.

São Paulo was originally a small Indian settlement, based on the lower terraces that rise from the **Rio Tiete**. Under the Portuguese Jesuit missionaries, the community grew slowly, serving only 300 inhabitants by the end of the sixteenth century. In the seventeenth century, settlers from Southern Portugal began to settle in São Paulo, using it as a base for expeditions into what later became Brazilian territory.

São Paulo saw its first massive European immigration after 1880. Attracted by the success of coffee cultivation, people came from Italy, Portugal, Germany, the Middle East and Asia. Today, São Paulo has the largest **Japanese population** of any community outside of Japan. This new, cosmopolitan population transformed the colonial São Paulo into a brilliant, independent-minded city.

Both the **Faculdade de Direito** (1827), the city's law school, and the **Universidade de São Paulo** (1934) increased São Paulo's reputation for intellectual and cultural excellence. The **Modern Art movement** took off in 1922, when the city hosted its first **Modern Art Week**, in which writers, artists and musicians gathered in the **Teatro Municipal**, bringing modern influences to the existing art community. Since 1951, São Paulo has hosted an international art show biannually, carrying on the strong artistic tradition in Brazil.

On original settlement's site, São Paulo's powerful business core has grown into an international presence, featuring its **Triangulo,** which is punctuated by the forty-two-story **Edificio Italia**.

São Paulo rests in the hills of the **Serra do Mar,** which is surrounded by open country and falls down the alluvial banks of three rivers. The wealthier populace builds their residences atop the gentle foothills of crystalline rock and red clay, while the riverbanks are inhabited by working class families and industrial buildings of manufacturing and commercial enterprises.

São Paulo skyline at night.

Sarajevo, a city with a cosmopolitan flavor and beautiful setting, has unfortunately suffered deeply in the twentieth century as both the flashpoint and battleground of major armed conflicts. Today it is the capital of the **Republic of Bosnia-Hercegovina**. The republic was part of the **Austro-Hungarian Empire** until 1918, part of a kingdom controlled by **Serbia** until 1929 and part of the Serbian-dominated **Republic of Yugoslavia** until 1992. In that year, Yugoslavia disintegrated into five republics fighting freedom from Serbia, or "rump" Yugoslavia. In 1994, this war has focused on Sarajevo, which at this writing is protected by the **United Nations'** peace keepers under British military leadership.

Sarajevo has always been considered one of the world's most culturally rich, enlightened cities due to its history of peaceful relations between ethnically and religiously diverse communities. Unfortunately, the city stands to lose both its fragile peace and its status as a community model for the rest of the world.

Sarajevo sits in a narrow valley along the **Milijacka River**. With only a few Roman relics, its old world character has been enhanced by local metalworkers and carpet makers. Though it grew into a center for commerce, intellectualism and tourism, the Muslim city preserves the feel of its ancestry. It retains the mosques, ornate wooden houses, marketplaces and public baths that are characteristic of Muslim cities. Until the war, the 1991 population of 526,000 was nearly one-half Muslim.

When the city was chosen as the site for the 1984 **Winter Olympic Games**, it was regarded as a cosmopolitan center where all nationalities were respected as they mingled in a community knit together by Serbs, Croats and Bosnian Muslims.

The city's Muslim character developed after the Turkish invasion of the late fifteenth century. The city grew into a successful Turkish trading post, and in the mid-sixteenth century the principal mosques (**Gazi Husreff-Bey's Mosque** and the **Mosque of Ali Pasha**) were built. Latin and Jewish quarters emerged, but in 1697, the whole city was burned by **Prince Eugene of Savoy**. In 1878, the Austro-Hungarian Empire ousted the Turks and annexed Bosnia and Hercegovina.

In Sarajevo in June 1914, a Bosnian Serb named **Gavril Princip** assassinated **Archduke Franz Ferdinand**, who was in line for the Empire's throne. This act mobilized Austro-Hungary against Serbia, which resulted in Imperial Russia coming to Serbia's aid, which touched off the tragic chain of events that led to **World War I**. In **World War II**, Sarajevo was quickly taken by the Germans, but guerrillas in the surrounding hills continued to resist. After the war, former guerrilla leader **Josip Broz Tito** transformed Yugoslavia into a Communist Republic. His death in 1980 led to a revolving presidency within the republics. In 1991, the federation began to dissolve as old ethnic rivalries boiled over.

As one of **Spain's** most precious centers for literature, education and the arts, **Seville** has a international reputation for its golden age of **literary salons**, its tiled and fountained patios, its whitewashed, balconied houses on small, shady streets and its annual **Six Day Fair**, called "the greatest fair in Europe," where gypsies and bullfighters in brightly adorned costumes can be seen alongside great horsemen and passionate **flamenco** dancers. The fair is held immediately after **Holy Week**, when processions of religious practitioners carry their statues of Christ and the Virgin Mary through the city's streets.

Seville's charms are natural as well as cultural. Located on the **Guadalquivir River** and among bounteous vineyards and orange groves, Seville's abundance beckons even the most pious. **St. Terese** was noted as saying that she had difficulty praying in Seville. "I did not recognize myself," she wrote. "There the devils have more hands with which to lead one into temptation."

Known as "the Spanish Athens," Seville saw its greatest days in the sixteenth century. Its greatest building, the **Seville Cathedral** (1519), is bigger and grander than any church except **St. Peter's** in Rome. As the city grew, neighborhoods of palaces and slums, both in the classic Spanish style, developed side by side. The learned aristocrats of Seville's culture built their lovely courtyards of red brick and tile, adorning them with myrtle, lilies and lemon and fig trees. The nobles patronized the city's poets and painters and built vast libraries. Meanwhile, an underworld of impoverished thieves turned into a well-manicured mafia that functioned in both the dirty streets of poor neighborhoods and the homes of the wealthy.

Pierre Chaunu has called the seventeenth century in Seville "an endless search for God," as convents, charitable works and baroque churches multiplied.

Seville has not developed into a great industrial city, although Spain offered it a monopoly on American trade in 1503. Poverty and sloth led to the city's decline throughout the eighteenth and nineteenth centuries. Unfortunately, this continued into the twentieth century, when **General Francisco Franco** and city officials decided to destroy early Seville's palaces and fine homes and build bland "modern" buildings, many of which are ugly.

In 1992, this city of 659,000 became a focal point for Europe and the world when it hosted both the **Olympic Games** and the World's Fair, called **Expo '92**, which celebrated the 500th anniversary of **Christopher Columbus'** voyage to America.

The colonnade of the Hall of Ambassadors in the Alcazar at Seville, circa 1930.

Now **China's** main industrial center, **Shanghai** was an agricultural town that was chosen to be the first Chinese city to open its port to Western trade. It developed into both one of the world's most successful seaports and most populated urban areas. Shanghai's healthy economy has been bettered further by an industrial base that uses its highly-skilled, innovative work force, its solidly based scientific research establishment and its excellent communication networks to compete with other twentieth century industrial giants. But greatness has its price. With a population of 7.5 million, Shanghai is now suffering the effects of major air, water and noise pollution. The **Wu-sung Chiang** (River) and **Huang-p'u Chiang**, which run through the mainland city, are clogged with industrial and domestic waste.

Shanghai's municipality covers 2,838 square miles (6,185 square kilometers), including nine mainland counties and approximately thirty islands in the **East China Sea**. The old Chinese city retains its random, winding street pattern and is surrounded by the grided streets of the modern city. Western Shanghai is mainly residential, and to the southwest is the Hsu-hui district, where **Jesuit priests** established libraries and a meteorological observatory in the 1800s.

Shanghai, like other southern Chinese cities, saw its first population boom when northern Chinese fled the **Mongols**, who were invading from the north. The new settlers inhabited Shanghai's self-sustaining agricultural lands, with the deep-watered port helping to stimulate a growing economy. In 1842, the **Treaty of Nanking**, which opened the city to unrestricted foreign trade, led to control of the city's commerce by foreign interests operating outside Chinese law in the European commercial district called **the Bund**. The city became a European bank hub, and foreign investments poured into Shanghai. Local investment was minimal until **World War I** diverted foreign funds, inviting Chinese investors into the market.

In 1921, the **Chinese Communist Party** was founded in Shanghai, leading to the "**May 30th**" uprising of 1925, but the Nationalist Government under **Chiang Kai-shek** suppressed the Communist movement. Japan occupied the city from 1937 to 1945, during both the **Sino-Japanese War** and **World War II**. The postwar period saw a civil war between Nationalists and Communists, and Shanghai, like all of China, fell to the latter in 1949. In the 1950s, Shanghai reemerged as China's leading scientific and technological research center.

Universities, including **Fu-tan, Chiao-t'ung** and **T'ung-chi**, are joined by cultural resources like the **Shanghai Museum of Art and History**, with its ancient bronze and ceramic artifacts, the **Shanghai Revolutionary History Memorial Hall**, which immortalizes the city's battles, and **Ta Shih-chieh**, the leading theater which features dance, folk opera and plays.

The port of Shanghai in the 1920s.

Singapore, long the linchpin of the **British Empire** in the Far East and now the capital of the **Republic of Singapore**, is a city-state located at the tip of the **Maylay Peninsula**. The city has been one of the world's most important ports practically since **Sir Stamford Raffles** first established a trading post here in 1819.

The city of Singapore, located on the southern coast of Singapore Island, has an area of 37 square miles (93 square kilometers). In the nineteenth century, it grew into a cosmopolitan center as Chinese, Malay and Indian immigrants came looking for economic opportunity.

Within the city's individual cultural enclaves and modern estates, the original settlement, where Raffles first landed, remains the city's center. Its public and government buildings, its **Anglican Cathedral** (1862) and its new skyscrapers all mix with the multi-ethnic styles that remain from the tides of Asian immigration. Known as "the **Garden City**" for its many parks and tree-lined streets, Singapore hosts such beauties as the **Tiger Balm Gardens**, which feature statuary depicting the mythical characters of Chinese legend, **Jurong Bird Park,** which covers fifty acres (20 hectares), and **Sentosa Island**, which was developed as a major recreational area.

Singapore was the most important city in the British Empire, its key to all the Far Eastern trade routes. The Japanese invaded in 1942, leading to what Britain's **Prime Minister Sir Winston Churchill** called "the worst disaster and largest capitulation in British history."

Singapore gained full independence in 1965, and from 1962 to 1982, the city maintained a 7.4 percent growth rate, one of the world's highest. By the early 1970s, Singapore was one of the Far East's most economically successful centers.

Singapore's success is due partly to its authoritarian leader, **Lee Kuan Yew**, who is known for his fastidious habits which have earned the city-state a reputation as Asia's best-ordered city, but one bent on enforcing intrusive family planning and a neatness policy that makes selling chewing gum illegal. Because of such strenuous control, Singapore's air and water are exceptionally clean, crime is at the barest minimum and the trash man visits each of its 2.8 million people's residences seven days a week.

Singapore in the early twentieth century.

Stockholm, Sweden's capital that has a population of 685,000, spans a number of islands in **Lake Malar**. About fifty bridges connect these islands with one another and to the mainland. Stockholm governs and dominates the cultural and educational life of Sweden, attracting some of the nation's finest artists and students. **Stockholm University** (1877) is joined by innumerable scientific academies and historical societies, and the **Nobel Prizes** (with the exception of the **Nobel Peace Prize**) are presented here each year.

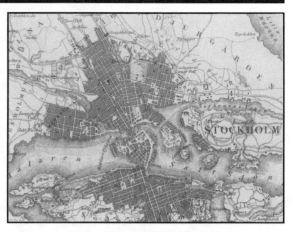

Map of Stockholm, circa 1850.

Stockholm's early growth of the thirteenth century, under the hand of **Birger Jarl**, was decided when the German city of **Lubeck** was offered a trade pact that involved no customs charges. The growth of trade brought new citizens to the flourishing city, which grew powerful under Sweden's **Sten Sture the Younger.** Some of Stockholm's most vicious history surrounds the years before **Gustav I Vasa** liberated Stockholm in 1523.

In 1520, Denmark's **Christian II** invaded Sweden and fought and killed the ruling Sten Sture. Swedish senators then agreed to place the Danish conqueror on the throne. While Christian signed a statement agreeing that he would rule by Swedish custom, Sture's widow, **Dame Christina Gyllenstjerna**, rallied the peasants of Stockholm to revolt and they beat the Danes at **Balundsas**. A month later, in a narrow victory at **Uppsala**, Christian again seized Stockholm and forced Christina to surrender. Christian was crowned King of Sweden in Stockholm's grand cathedral, and on the third night of celebration, Danish soldiers seized some of the Swedish guests. Two bishops were charged that night with heresy and executed the next evening at midnight. The Danes went on to slaughter 80 other Swedish noblemen, and Christian imprisoned Dame Christina, burned the body of Sture and suppressed all opposition.

One of the victims, **Erik Vasa**, had a son, **Gustavus Eriksson**, who heard of King Christian's bloody crowning after he escaped from Christian's **fortress of Kalo**, where he had been held for a year. Eriksson, learning that the new king wanted him killed, rallied the yeomen into a force that drove the Danes out of Sweden. Gustav I Vasa subsequently became Sweden's ruler, while Stockholm became its capital.

The city then developed rapidly, and the city center, called **Gamla Stan**, contains some of the era's finest buildings. These include the **Royal Palace**, the **Cathedral of St. Nicholas** and the **House of Lords**, which are on **Stads Island**, the lovely **Riddarholm Church**, which is on **Riddar Island**, and the **House of Parliament** and the **National Bank**, which are on **Helgeands Island**.

The city was modernized by the **Industrial Revolution** that developed metal and machinery manufacturing as well as the paper and printing industries. In 1912, Stockholm was chosen to host the **Olympic Games**, and the city's **T-line subway** (1950) has 94 modern stations and 60 miles of track.

Sydney evolved from a penal colony that was populated by British convicts. Some offenses committed by Sydney's first citizens were very slight, such as stealing a handkerchief or borrowing a glove. Out of respect, throughout all of January Sydney still celebrates the January 26th, 1788 landing, when the first convicts were dropped off near the current downtown area.

Sydney, the capital of the **New South Wales** state, is **Australia's** oldest and largest city. Its vast metropolitan area covers 4,790 square miles (12,407 square kilometers), spanning from the **Blue Mountains** in the west to the **Pacific Ocean** in the east. Sydney's 1990 population was 3.7 million, which is more than ten times its 1890 citizenry of 220,000. The city is known to have one of the world's best ports, as **Captain Arthur Phillip** discovered in 1788 when he reached **Port Jackson**. After having first sailed to **Botany Bay** (located immediately south of Sydney's site), which had been discovered and settled by **Captain John Cook** in 1770, Phillip noted the Port Jackson's excellent natural harbor and moved the entire fleet.

Innumerable coves and bays are found on the Pacific coast near Sydney, along with exquisite beaches that are world renowned for surfing and boating. Australians are great lovers of the outdoors, and there are two magnificent national parks within 25 miles of the city center.

Though the city's architecture is modern and fairly unremarkable, Sydney is dominated by two exceptional landmarks. The first is the **Sydney Harbour Bridge** (1933), which arcs high behind the Opera House and links the north shore to the city. The second is the **Opera House** (1973), designed by Danish architect **Jorn Utzon**, which houses a concert hall for the **Sydney Symphony Orchestra** as well as a large theater for opera and ballet and a smaller theater for plays. The Opera House is linked to **Hyde Park** by **Macquarie Street**, which is lined magnificently with nineteenth century government buildings. Like its rival **Melbourne**, which once bested this city in population and importance, Sydney has a few delicate, lacy iron balconies that add florid decoration to the city's buildings.

Like all Australians, many of Sydney's citizens have become great historical researchers, collecting all evidence of its early settlement and tracing their roots through the generations of the city's short life. Though founded by convicts and peopled by women who were badly abused at their arrival, Sydney also attracted citizens who came because the British government was providing free land, convict labor and free capital works. The city still remembers the adventurous spirit of its early settlers.

Sydney's famous Opera House.

The largest city on the island of **Taiwan** (formerly **Formosa**), **Taipei** bills itself as the capital of the **Republic of China**, an exiled political entity that considers itself the legitimate government of all of mainland China. After they won China's civil war (1945-1949), the Communists set up the **People's Republic of China** to rule the mainland. Meanwhile, the Chinese Nationalists — who had ruled China since 1912 — escaped to Taiwan, and under its president, **Chiang Kai-shek**, set up the present exile government, which was recognized as the legitimate by the rest of the world community until 1971, when the People's Republic was given the "China" seat in the **United Nations**.

Taipei is a fairly young city sitting on the former sites of rice and vegetable farms that flourished in the **Tanshui River's** fertile valley before the eighteenth century. The city's heart lies in the center, called **Old Taipei**, while to the east, in **New Taipei**, modern buildings of glass and steel spring up continually. Massive construction of commercial and residential buildings, as well as a gigantic new subway system, contributes to the noise and traffic.

Taipei saw its first population explosion in the early nineteenth century. One hundred and twenty-one miles southeast of China's mainland, across the **Taiwan Straight**, it became an important center for overseas trade. In 1895, after the **Sino-Japanese War**, Japan acquired the island (then known as Formosa) and made Taipei (then known as Tamsui) the capital. Japan's defeat in **World War II** gave the island back to China.

Politics aside, Taipei is a booming industrial city on the island's northern tip. Hosting most of Taiwan's important textile factories, as well as its shipbuilding, electronic and canned goods factories, Taipei continues to grow at excessive speed, despite efforts to establish new industries and educational institutions elsewhere.

Today, the metropolitan area spans 138 square miles (357 square kilometers) and houses over 2.7 million people. The city is connected to all of Taiwan via railways and bus lines, and to the rest of the world through the **Chiang Kai-shek International Airport**. The **National Taiwan University** (1928), the **National Taiwan Normal University** (1946) and the **National Chengcha University** (1927) all exist in Taipei, as does the **National Palace Museum**, which houses the world's largest collection of ancient Chinese artifacts, including priceless porcelain, calligraphy and paintings.

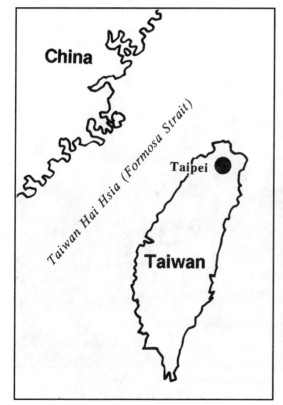

The city of **Teheran**, whose population today numbers six million, is built on the southern slopes of the **Elburz Mountains**, about 62 miles (100 kilometers) south of the **Caspian Sea**. It sits between the **Jajrud** and **Karat rivers,** where it was once a suburb of the ancient capital, **Rayy,** that was destroyed by **Mongol warriors** in 1220 AD.

Its capture in 1785 led Teheran to its current wealth and prominence. Teheran was made the capital of **Persia** in 1788 by its vicious captor, **Agha Mohammad Khan,** who founded the **Qajar Dynasty** that ruled **Persia** until 1925, when the government was seized by **General Reza Pahlavi**, who made himself the Shah, or monarch. In 1935, Persia was renamed as **Iran.**

As the capital of Persia, and then Iran, Teheran first achieved international prominence in 1943, during **World War II**, when it hosted the first summit conference of the "Big Three" Allied leaders, **Joseph Stalin, Winston Churchill** and **Franklin D. Roosevelt**.

The son of the original Shah, also named Reza Pahlavi, imagined his monarchy to be the inheritor of the glory of 6,000 years of imperial Persia. During the 1970s, he used revenues from Iran's oil wealth to turn Teheran into a glittering showplace city that emulated Europe's capitals.

In 1979, however, growing unrest among Iran's Islamic fundamentalists forced the Shah from power, and the **Islamic Republic of Iran** was established. Under this strict theocracy, Teheran's image shifted dramatically, becoming much more somber and forcing European-style amusements, such as bars and nightclubs, to close.

Nevertheless, Teheran remains an economically important city, where half of Iran's manufactured goods are now produced. The **University of Tehran**, the **National University of Iran** and the **Arya Mehr University of Technology** all exist within the city's 112 square miles (290 square kilometers).

The **old town**, populated since at least 3,000 BC, and the original bazaar still function in the south. **Niavaran Palace** still stands, as well as the **Golestan Palace**, the **Sa'adabad** and the **Marmar**, which have all been converted into museums.

The government gate at Teheran is a beautiful example of Persian architecture.

Tel Aviv was founded as the first all-Jewish city in what is now **Israel**. Late in the nineteenth century, the **Second Aliya**, a middle class Jewish refugee movement fleeing Russian anti-Semitism, moved to **Palestine**, then a vilayet (province) of the Turkish **Ottoman Empire**. They landed in the Mediterranean port city of **Jaffa** (or **Yafa**), which had been a **Canaanite city** taken by **Egypt** in the fifteenth century. They proceeded to set up a Jewish social structure on Jaffa's edge that would eventually evolve into Tel Aviv.

In 1917, after the defeat of the Ottoman Empire in **World War I**, Britain took control of Palestine and British Foreign Secretary **Arthur Balfour** proposed the establishment of a Jewish state in the region. This idea was taken up by the **United Nations** after **World War II**, and the modern state of Israel came into being, with Tel Aviv as its first capital.

In the meantime, a large Jewish immigrant population had swelled Tel Aviv's population from 1,000 in 1917 to 160,000 in 1947. Though Jaffa declined, Tel Aviv, which had 353,000 citizens by 1990, grew into a modern metropolis where more than half of Israel's industry is found.

Tel Aviv, like nearby **Jerusalem**, has often been a battleground in the violent conflict between the state of Israel and various Palestinian groups who wish to see the establishment of a Palestinian state on Israeli land. The city was also a target of ballistic missile attacks, which were launched from Iraq during the 1991 **Persian Gulf War**.

Not only does the city support Israel's banks, insurance companies and its only stock exchange, Tel Aviv preserves its nation's cultural heritage. The **Israel Philharmonic Orchestra**, the **Chamber Ensemble**, the **Israeli Opera** and over a dozen theaters function in Tel Aviv, as do several **rabbinical institutes, Tel Aviv University** and the **Bar-Ilan University**.

An early view of the city of Tel Aviv.

Tokyo, Japan's current capital and largest city, has been called "the city of contrasts" and "the capital of old and new" or, as **Donald Richie** suggests in his book, *A Lateral View,* "mod but trad." With streets that sometimes fit no pattern and have no names, small, perfect gardens that feature lillied lakes, and castles that are surrounded by many moats, Tokyo has preserved some of its most peaceful spaces in the midst of one of the world's busiest, most powerful commercial centers. By the 1980s, the world's largest banks were Japanese, and Tokyo accordingly grew into a bustling financial capital. Today, Tokyo's 1,089 square miles (2,820 square kilometers) are home to 8.1 million people, up from 1.2 million in 1890 and 6.8 million during **World War II**.

The city was called **Edo** until it was made Japan's capital in 1868. After ending the reign of the **Tokugawa Shogunate**, the young emperor **Mutsuhito** moved the capital out of **Kyoto** and into Edo, which he renamed Tokyo, meaning "eastern capital." Edo was founded at the mouth of the **Sumida River** and has now become the inner portion of Tokyo. It was originally dominated by the **Castle of Edo**, which has since burned down and been replaced by the **Imperial Palace**. The new royal residence was built on the original castle grounds, which were fortified by moats rather than European style city walls, and was surrounded by gardens, as were other noble residences.

To the east of the Imperial Palace is **Marunouchi**, the thriving center of Japanese business, and to its south, the **Metropolitan Government Offices** lie across the moat from **Kanda**,

Tokyo's university and publishing center. In the western part of the city, foreign embassies share their quiet, residential streets with **Tokyo University, Waseda University** and **Keio University**. Nearly all of Japan's prefectures (provinces) have offices in the city, and many governmental associations are located in Tokyo.

Tokyo's style varies dramatically, sometimes from door to door. Although some traditional dwellings, including small wooden houses and shops fronting family residences, still exist, a lot of new construction has been done with materials like concrete and glass molded into sharp corners and smooth planes. Along with Tokyo's financial giants, a large portion of the city's businesses are small family shops with less than 30 workers, and many residents still temper their twentieth century tastes with traditional tatami mats and sliding doors.

The city holds national historical treasures in the **Tokyo National Museum** in **Ueno Park**, the **National Science Museum**, the **Zoological Museum** and the **National Museum of Western Art**. The **East Garden of the Imperial Palace** is now open for public view, and the **Meiji Shrine's Outer Garden** was one of the main centers for the **Olympic Games** in 1964.

An aerial view of Tokyo.

As **Ontario Province's** capital and **Canada's** largest city, **Toronto** stretches over 154 square miles (398 square kilometers) of lowlands that front **Lake Ontario** near the United States border. It is Canada's largest financial center and home to 3.9 million people, up from 181,000 in 1890.

After the American **War of Independence**, British loyalists fled north, where they established Toronto on a small trading post. The site was originally founded by French fur merchants before being taken over by the British in 1759, during the **French & Indian War.**

Toronto experienced an enormous rate of growth in the early twentieth century. In 1953, Metropolitan Toronto was established, linking the communities of **Etobicoke, North York** and **Scarborough** with Toronto in order to ensure successful city planning. Since then, Toronto has built an enormous underground city for its residents to enjoy, particularly during the painfully harsh winters. Government buildings, business offices, hotels and restaurants can now be reached without ever leaving the underground city.

Though Toronto remains a very safe, clean city, dominated by its twin towers and surrounded by rich, rolling farmland, it is no longer a quiet little town. Its metropolitan culture emerged in the 1950s, when Toronto absorbed a massive influx of postwar immigrants, made up of 300,000 Italians, 80,000 Greeks, plus Chinese, Hungarian and Portuguese peoples, each bringing their own cultural riches to Toronto's markets and neighborhoods.

Toronto: the CN tower, SkyDome stadium, and waterfront.

Tunis, modern **Tunisia's** capital city, evolved from and is built adjacent to the site of the ancient city of **Carthage**, which was once **Rome's** rival for political and economic supremacy in the **Mediterranean**. Begun as a Libyan settlement and surrendered to the **Phoenicians** in the ninth century BC, Carthage rose to economic prominence in the Mediterranean during the third century BC because the skilled shipbuilders and traders there added Greek pottery, Cyprus copper and Spanish silver to the Egyptian linen and Mediterranean slaves that Carthage already traded.

The city was built at the edge of a shallow lake, which is an inlet of the **Gulf of Tunis**. Lying off the coast of the Mediterranean Sea, the city not only enjoyed open trade routes, but maintained great olive groves and agricultural lands, which remain major staples of the national economy.

Conflict with the Roman Empire came in a series of three **Punic Wars** between 264 BC and 146 BC, resulting in both Carthage's defeat as an economic power and the destruction of the city itself. The city, which subsequently was used as a Roman outpost and still contains the magnificent ruins of the **aqueduct** that once linked the ancient Carthage to **Mount Zaghwan**, didn't reach its zenith until the thirteenth and fourteenth centuries. After the **Muslim conquest** of the seventh century, it was made the capital city of the **Aghlabids** between 800 and 909. Beginning in 1236, the city also enjoyed a period of great prosperity under the **Hafsid Dynasty**. The Romans, under the Holy Roman Emperor **Charles V**, took possession of Tunis again in 1535, but the powerful Ottoman Turks captured the city in 1539, only to lose it to the Spaniards, who held Tunis from 1573 to 1574 but yielded it back to the Turks, who remained in control until the French protectorate (1881-1956). The Germans took Tu-

A street scene in Tunis.

nis during **World War II**, it was liberated by the British in 1943, and in 1956, it became the capital of independent Tunisia.

Some evidence of Tunis's historical greatness remains in the old city's buildings, like the eighth century **Mosque of Az-Zaytunah**, which is venerated as the oldest surviving mosque in Tunisia, and the second century **thermal baths**, which were built under Rome's **Antonine emperors**. The city has grown during the twentieth century from 145,000 people in 1890 to 835,000 in 1990. During this time the city has added important institutions, like the **University of Tunis** (1960), thermoelectric plants and international airports, which help it survive in an age of greater mobility, increased tourism and industrial competition.

Vancouver, on the southwestern coast of **British Columbia**, is **Canada's** main Pacific port. It is also home to 1.6 million people — half the entire population of British Columbia — up from a mere 14,000 in 1890. Surrounded on three sides by water, with snowy peaks rising to the east, Vancouver was settled on one of the world's most lovely, wooded sites. It faces the **Georgia Straight** to the west, across which lies **Vancouver Island**.

Beginning as the sawmill settlement of **Granville** in the 1870s, Vancouver's ice-free port made it an excellent terminus for the **Canadian Pacific Railroad**. Trade was also aided by the **Panama Canal**, which facilitated easier sea transportation for Vancouver with eastern Canada, American East Coast ports and Europe. By the 1930s, the city had grown into the third largest in Canada, covering 44 square miles (114 square kilometers).

Since the 1960s, high-rise buildings and neatly kept city parks have given Vancouver a vital urban core to complement its rich cosmopolitan personality. Such charms, along with a powerful economy stimulated by the excellent opportunities of the city's natural deep water port, have made Vancouver the choicest spot for British Columbia's industrial, financial and commercial center, as well as for **Expo '86**, the 1986 World's Fair.

Vancouver, like many Canadian cities, houses a racially diverse population. The **Chinatown** district is one of the Pacific Coast's largest, second only to that of **San Francisco**. In the nineteenth and twentieth centuries, **Sikhs** from the **Punjab**, along with many others from the Indian subcontinent, came to work in the sawmills, where they managed the logs of a booming lumber industry. Thanks to encouraging tax incentives, Vancouver is now the filming site for a great many American films and television series. While the city is used to represent American locations, its distinct skyline can often be anonymously identified in the background.

The Vancouver skyline, as seen from the water.

Venice is considered the most romantic of Europe's great cities, with its labyrinthine streets that allow no cars, its lacquered **gondolas** and poetic **gondoliers** on the inky waters of serpentine canals, its overflowing flower boxes, its **Gothic palaces** and its glass factories that produce handblown delicacies.

Venice is a city of islands bisected by the famous canals that are the primary avenues of transportation for its 306,000 residents. The city is ruled by water. Lying on an archipelago at the northwestern end of the **Adriatic Sea**, Venice sits in a crescent-shaped lagoon protected by sandbanks. Even with this protection, floods have been disastrous in recent years, and now the **United Nations Educational, Scientific, and Cultural Organization (UNESCO)** is coordinating an international program to save the city from the combined effects of corrosive air pollution, further flooding and simple age.

Founded after the collapse of the **Roman Empire** as an island fortress city, Venice was never captured by the northern European hordes that brought down the Empire. It was subsequently claimed by the **Eastern Roman**, or **Byzantine Empire**, but was in reality a self-governing republic under the **doges** (dukes), whose pink stone palace is one of the city's wonders. Venice became the dominant city-state in the Adriatic and competed with the Byzantines for Mediterranean supremacy. In the ninth century, doges were chosen by popular election, and in the eleventh, **Alexius I Comnenus** granted Venice unrestricted trade throughout the Byzantine Empire in gratitude for her help against the **Normans**.

Venetians were excellent enterprisers and in the **Fourth Crusade**, the Venetian doge was one of the leaders of the sacking of the Byzantine city of **Constantinople**, which left Venice with a powerful commercial empire. It wasn't until 1261 that the emperor in exile recovered Constantinople and granted important trade rights in the Black Sea to **Genoa**, making that city Venice's chief rival. In 1508, after three centuries as the key power in the region, Venice was defeated by Spanish, French and German forces aligned with the pope, Hungarians and Savoyards. The last doge was abdicated in 1797, when the city became part of **Napoleon's** French Empire. Venice later became part of Austria until 1866, when it became part of a unified **Italy**.

The city's architectural treasures — such as its splendid homes and the **Cathedral of San Marco** on the **Piazza San Marco** — date from its golden age, but great artists — from **Antonio Vivaldi** in the eighteenth century to **Renaissance** painters **Giovanni Bellini, Giorgione** and **Titian** — have worked here throughout history.

Although it is now fighting the effects of age and rising waters, Venice conveys the illusion of a city nearly untouched by the modern world, the ultimate walking city with the romantic offerings of evening gondola rides and the discovery of hidden piazzi and tiny private canals.

The canals of Venice.

Vienna, on the banks of the **Danube**, Europe's great river, is **Austria's** capital and largest city, as well as one of Europe's cultural diamonds. Vienna is cherished for its musical masters and their artistic contributions. Composers **Franz Josef Haydn** and **Franz Schubert** were both members of the **Vienna Boys' Choir** (1498). **Wolfgang Amadeus Mozart** and **Ludwig von Beethoven** both premiered some of their finest works in the **Theater an der Wien**. **Giuseppe Verdi** and **Richard Wagner** both conducted at the **Vienna State Opera** (1869), which opened with a performance of Mozart's **Don Giovanni** and, after its **World War II** destruction, reopened in 1955 with Beethoven's **Fidelio**.

In the twentieth century, Vienna gave rise to the artists who broke with tradition, like **Gustav Klimt** and **Alfred Kubin**, and to the masters of the **Art Nouveau** and **Fantastic Realism** schools. Vienna was also home to such diverse figures as **Sigmund Freud, Theodor Herzl**, the founder of **Zionism**, and **Adolf Hitler**.

Vienna, an important trading city during and after the **Roman Empire**, became an important political center under the dynasty of the **Hapsburgs**, who came to power in 1276 and ruled for over 600 years. Even as the Hapsburgs built a great empire that stretched from Turkey to Italy, Vienna was a city where the arts were greatly supported, especially by **Maria Theresa**, who ruled in the late eighteenth century.

Napoleon occupied Vienna in 1805, and again in 1809. By 1814, the **Congress of Vienna** was involved in Europe's restoration. The Hapsburg monarchy fell after **World War I**, and the Republic of Austria was born in 1918, with Vienna as the capital. **Marxists** and conservative opponents rallied in the streets, and in 1933, an authoritarian regime, formed by the Austrian chancellor, **Engelbert Dollfuss,** assumed power. Hitler, after convincing Austrians that they were a historically German people, easily absorbed Austria into Germany in 1938, stripping Vienna of its position. Vienna lost an enormous number of its Jewish citizens during **World War II**. At the war's end, Vienna was taken by **Soviet troops**. The city and the nation were subsequently occupied by the Allied forces, who withdrew in 1955 under the **Austrian State Treaty**, making Vienna once again the capital city of an independent Austria.

Today Vienna is a city of 1.6 million — compared to 1.4 million at the end of the Hapsburg era — that spans an area of 160 square miles (415 square kilometers). In recent years, Vienna attracted international conferences to its **Vienna International Centre**, as well as the headquarters of some of the world's most important organizations: the **International Atomic Energy Agency**, the **Organization of Petroleum Exporting Countries (OPEC)**, and the **United Nations Industrial Development Organization**.

The Schoenbrunn Castle, Vienna.

Warsaw, Poland's capital and cultural center, has witnessed some of the greatest heroic tragedies of the twentieth century. After centuries of being attacked and dominated by either Russians or Germans, Warsaw became the capital of an independent Poland after **World War I**, only to be blasted to ruins by both Nazi Germany and the Soviet Union in **World War II**. The city also witnessed the near destruction of its entire Jewish population in 1944, when German troops led a massacre of its remaining **Warsaw ghetto** citizens — many had been shipped already to the **Auschwitz** and **Treblinka** death camps — while Russian troops stood by and watched.

A small trading settlement in the tenth century, Warsaw was made the capital of the **Duchy of Mazovia** in the fifteenth century, and New Town sprang up around the original settlement, called Old Town. In 1526, Warsaw became capital of the **Kingdom of Poland**, which was conquered by Sweden in 1655.

Under Russian, Prussian and — briefly — Napoleonic domination after the **War of the Polish Succession** (1733-1738), Warsaw became "the capital without a country," but flourished as cultural center until 1863, when a revolt against the Russians resulted in a crackdown that included banning the speaking of the Polish language.

Between the World Wars, Warsaw, as capital of a free Poland, experienced a cultural renaissance. With censorship at a minimum and a large number of great minds flooding the city for its cultural flavor, Warsaw established the **International Chopin Competition for Pianists** (1927) and the **Henryk Wieniawski International Violin Competition** (1935). It supported flamboyant performers, such as **Hanka Ordonowna** and **Ida Kaminska**, playwrights, like **George Bernard Shaw**, and writers, like **Zofia Nalkowska** and **Czeslaw Milosz**, who later won the Nobel Prize for Literature.

The Communist party ruled Poland from 1947 to 1989, when **Solidarity**, an independent party that evolved from an autonomous labor union, won 99 of 100 senate seats. Solidarity leader **Wojciech Jaruzelski** was elected president by the parliament, and Poland began the transition to a free market economy, which was heartily welcomed by Warsaw's entrepreneurs.

Warsaw today bears almost no resemblance to the city that endured such heavy shelling during World War II, though some exquisite buildings remain — among them the Gothic **St. John's Cathedral** and the **Church of the Holy Christ**, which contains **Frederick Chopin's** heart — and the **Old Town Market Square** has been rebuilt to mirror its fifteenth century style. The **Church of St. Alexander** is a remnant of the tsarist era, and the **Royal Castle**, an excellent example of eighteenth century style, lords over **Zamkowy Square**.

Divided into right and left bank districts by the **Vistula River,** Warsaw is home to 1.7 million people — compared to 456,000 in 1890 — and the city covers an area of 174 square miles (450 square kilometers).

The historic city hall of Warsaw, circa 1920.

As the **United States'** capital, **Washington DC** is home to the executive, judicial and legislative branches of government, making it the political power center of the world's richest nation. It is also one of the nation's biggest tourist attractions, due largely to the **Smithsonian Institution** complex, the world's largest and most-visited museum.

The White House, Washington DC.

The 357 square mile (896 square kilometer) metropolis of Washington DC was planned by French architect and artist **Pierre-Charles L'Enfant** with the help of **George Washington**. The nation's first president was responsible for choosing the site, located on the **Potomac River,** as the perfect spot for the nation's grand capital, the **District of Columbia (DC)**. The District once contained several cities, but they are now contiguous with Washington.

The centerpiece of Washington is the **Capital Mall**, a three-mile strip of grass that stretches from the **Lincoln Memorial**, which overlooks the Potomac, to **Capitol Hill**. The **United States Capitol Building** sits atop Capitol Hill, where it is both dominated by and offers a view of the 555-foot **Washington Monument**. The Mall is bordered by the nine major Smithsonian buildings that include the **National Gallery of Art**, the **National Museum of Natural History**, the **National Museum of American History** and the **National Air and Space Museum**.

The executive mansion of the president, the **White House**, is six blocks north of the Washington Monument, and the area between the two structures and the Capitol is known as the **Federal Triangle**. Around the Capitol are clustered the **Supreme Court**, several congressional office buildings and the **Library of Congress**. L'Enfant's original desires for the magnificent city of Washington included its status as a cultural capital, which was not realized until recently. In the mid-twentieth century, major memorials, like the **John F. Kennedy Center for the Performing Arts**, were created as functional buildings that could serve artistic purposes as well.

Ford's Theatre, where **President Abraham Lincoln** was assassinated, has been renovated, and the **National Gallery of Art** has gained international recognition for its collection of world masters. Washington's **Arena Stage** (1950) has gained prestige since it was founded, and the **National Symphony Orchestra** has been growing into a well-respected body. An area of the city, **Georgetown**, is home to the **Georgetown School of Law** and **Georgetown University**.

While the District's population — which has grown from 230,000 in 1890 to 607,000 in 1990 — maintains high rankings as having one of the nation's greatest percentages of college educated citizens and also one of the nation's highest per capita income levels, its ranks still contribute to the city's high crime rate and large pockets of poverty and unemployment.

Wellington is the capital and second largest city in **New Zealand**, which was the first nation to give women the vote in 1893. Surrounding **Port Nicholson**, one of the world's fine harbors, Wellington overlooks the **Cook Strait**, which separates New Zealand's **North** and **South islands.** The city's location, which is midway between **Auckland**, the nation's largest city, and **Christchurch**, its third largest, enables Wellington to act as a player in both domestic and international trade.

The city's original settlement began at the mouth of the **Hutt River**. Two British ships that landed in 1826 settled the site in order to collect timber. The **New Zealand Company** arrived in 1839, colonizing a small area of the **Hutt River Valley** to serve as its first company settlement. When the Hutt River Valley was declared unsuitable, the New Zealand Company's site was moved to **Lambton Harbor** on the west shore of North Island. Named in recognition of the first **Duke of Wellington** during its formal annexation by Britain in 1840, the city began to expand, growing into a borough in 1842 and a municipality in 1853. In 1865, the government of New Zealand — which was granted self-governing status in 1852 — was moved from Auckland to Wellington.

The municipality now includes the cities of **Lower Hutt, Upper Hutt** and **Porirua**. Since the 1950s, the valley, once thought unsuitable for anything but dairy farms and market gardens, has absorbed most of the city's urban overflow. With 327,000 residents ringing Port Nicholson and investing in the industrial future of their city, Wellington continues to expand its commercial and financial base.

As the nation's hub of commerce and transportation, Wellington hosts its international airport, its rail and road services that extend to all parts of North Island as well as the ferry service that links North Island to South Island.

The city not only enjoys the cosmopolitan lifestyle of great port cities, but an excellent physical environment as well. Lying on the extreme south of North Island, it occupies the shores and hills of Port Nicholson. Much of the city's 532 square mile (1,379 square kilometers) area sits on land reclaimed from the bay.

The city is dominated by **Mount Victoria,** which rises 643 feet from the city's center. Around it are buildings such as the **National Art Gallery**, the **Dominion Museum**, the **Parliament buildings**, and the **Victory University** (1897). The **Old Government Building** (1876) is reputed to be one of the world's largest surviving wooden structures.

The port of Wellington in the 1920s.

Overlooking the beautiful **Zurich See** (lake), **Zurich, Switzerland's** largest city and home to a population of 345,000, is a world banking center, an industrial metropolis, and a hub for fine arts and crafts production. Zurich is the financial heart of Switzerland, which holds an international reputation for its banking laws that offer depositors a higher level of anonymity than any other nation.

The first inhabitants of Zurich were prehistoric people, who formed dwellings on the shores of **Lake Zurich**. The **Celtic Helvetii** built a settlement on the **Limmat River** bank, and the **Romans** held the community until their empire's collapse, when it passed to the **Alamanii**, and later to the **Franks**, who made it a royal residence. By 1218, its excellent position on European trade routes had established it as an imperial free city.

The **Swiss Protestant Reformation** was born in Zurich through the liberal preachings of **Huldrych Zwingli**, who, in the early sixteenth century, denounced Lenten fasting and insisted that the bishop of Constance allow his priests to marry. The city was drastically affected by his leadership, as well as by the **Counter-Reformation** that brought the **Catholic cantons** together against **Protestant Zurich**, which was defeated at the 1531 **battle of Kappel**, in which Zwingli was killed.

Industry has always been a powerful force, and by 1787, one quarter of Zurich's population worked in the textile mills, which developed from the city's medieval silk industry.

In the 1830s, a liberal democratic order helped Zurich's citizenry gain control of governmental decisions, and the city rose into the nineteenth and twentieth centuries with a healthy economy and a strong industrial base.

The **Swiss National Museum** (1898), which contains a collection of historical and artistic pieces, is a national treasure, as is the city itself, which holds priceless examples of historical architecture. The **Grossmunster** was built by **Charlemagne** in the eighth century, while **St. Peter's Church** dates back to the thirteenth century.

The city's operas and theaters were known worldwide for their innovation and experimental spirit during the nineteenth and twentieth centuries. The playful **Dada** artistic and literary movement got its start in Zurich in 1916, leading to the more popular **Surrealist** movement in 1917; both were ironic additions to the staid image of a banking city. The city's cultural energy grew incredibly, attracting artists like **Bertolt Brecht**, whose *Mother Courage* (1941) was produced at the **Schauspielhaus**. This same spirit enlivens the city's annual festivals, which are said to "loose the demons in men's hearts."

The Zurich skyline.

TRIVIA QUESTIONS & PROJECT SUGGESTIONS

1. Some cities use a system of canals the way others use a system of streets. Which cities use canals as a major mode of transportation? (See Nos. 2 Amsterdam, 7 Bangkok, 43 Jakarta, 95 Venice)

2. Some cities are still valuable cultural sites, even though they are no longer inhabited by civilizations. Which cities were rediscovered after their abandonment and are no longer inhabited? (See Nos. 3 Angkor, 55 Machu Picchu, 72 Pompeii)

3. Which city is located in both Asia and Europe, and was originally named Constantinople when it was founded as the "New Rome?" (See No. 42 Istanbul)

4. Which city was home to musical masters Wolfgang Mozart and Ludwig von Beethoven? (See No. 83 Vienna)

5. The British and Dutch East India Companies were powerful forces in the seventeenth and eighteenth centuries. Which cities came under the influence of the British East India Company? Which cities came under the influence of the Dutch East India Company? (See Nos. 19 Calcutta, 20 Canton, 21 Cape Town, 43 Jakarta, 85 Singapore)

6. Which cities came under the control of the Turks during the long-lived Ottoman Empire period? (See Nos. 1 Algiers, 6 Baghdad, 8 Barcelona, 10 Beirut, 18 Cairo, 26 Damascus 42 Istanbul, 44 Jerusalem, 82 Sarajevo, 93 Tunis)

7. The monuments and architectural wonders of the world's great cities are international treasures. Name five great monuments of either architectural or aesthetic fame. In what cities do they reside? (See Nos. 4 Athens, 52 London, 62 Moscow, 67 New York City, 70 Paris, 75 Rome, 78 San Francisco)

8. Which city is the spiritual home to three of the world's major religions? What three religions are they? (See No. 44 Jerusalem)

9. Which city was considered the richest city in the world during the eighth and ninth centuries? What famous book of stories was written about this city at its zenith? (See No. 6 Baghdad)

10. Which cities lie on the banks of the Nile River along with the ancient "city of the Dead" and the pyramids of the pharaohs? (See Nos. 18 Cairo, 54 Luxor)

11. Which city was founded by the fleeing Inca warriors who hid from the Spanish in the mountains, where the ruins of this city still lie? (See No. 55 Machu Picchu)

12. Which two, relatively modern, cities grew into powerful cultural centers when gold was discovered nearby? One is an American city and one is an African city. (See Nos. 45 Johannesburg and 78 San Francisco)

13. Which city was famous for the quality of its artists and scientists including Dante, Michelangelo, Galileo and Leonardo da Vinci? (See No. 31 Florence)

14. Which city was the center of the Calvinist Reformation of the sixteenth century? This city has become the world's center for important conferences, including meetings of several United Nations agencies. (See No. 32 Geneva)

15. Which city was traditionally called the automobile capital of the world? What else is it famous for? (See No. 28 Detroit)

16. Which city, founded as "the Capital of Peace and Tranquility," has become the national center for Buddhism and Japanese culture? (See No. 47 Kyoto)

17. The world's great museums are great resources for understanding cultural history. What city houses the world's largest museum complex? (See No. 98 Washington, DC).

18. Name at least three other cities that maintain great art museums. (See Nos. 2 Amsterdam, 52 London, 56 Madrid, 67 New York City, 69 Oslo, 70 Paris, 73 Prague, 75 Rome, 84 Shanghai)

19. Many cities gave rise to literary and artistic movements. Name some of the world's great writers and the cities they lived in. (See Nos. 4 Athens-Homer, Plato, Aristotle, 24 Chicago-Saul Bellow, Gwendolyn Brooks, Carl Sandburg, Theodore Dreiser, 52 London-Dickens, Shakespeare, 70 Paris-de Balzac, Collette, 78 San Francisco-Mark Twain)

20. Which city would you most like to visit and why?

21. If you had to write an essay on a city not included in this book, which one would you choose?

INDEX